A Stakeholder Approach to Issues Management

A Stakeholder Approach to Issues Management

Robert Boutilier

First published in 2011 by
Business Expert Press, LLC
222 East 46th Street, New York, NY 10017
www.businessexpertpress.com

ISBN-13: 978-1-60649-097-6 (paperback)

ISBN-13: 978-1-60649-098-3 (e-book)

DOI 10.4128/ 9781606490983

A publication in the Business Expert Press Strategic Management collection

Collection ISSN: 2150-9611 (print)
Collection ISSN: 2150-9646 (electronic)

Cover design by Jonathan Pennell
Interior design by Scribe Inc.

First edition: December 2011

10 9 8 7 6 5 4 3 2 1

Printed in the United States of America.

Abstract

A Stakeholder Approach to Issues Management offers a fact-based strategy development process for managing issues and controversies.

The book shows practitioners how to ground their strategic advice on empirical research that reveals the socio-political dynamics of the issue. It is the first book to approach issues management from a blended application of advances in stakeholder theory and social network analysis. Readers learn how to track the socio-political environment in order to (a) avoid risks and crises, (b) obtain essential environmental scanning information for strategy development or adjustment, and (c) secure the organization's reputation and access to vital resources.

The approach begins with the insight that stakeholders are embedded in networks that influence their stances on issues and shape the range of available coalitions they can form. Further, the issue concepts themselves are arranged in networks, with some concepts being pivotal to shifting the loyalties of whole sections of the stakeholder network. By analyzing the joint network structures of who-knows-whom and who-cares-about-what, managers can develop network intervention strategies that move everyone towards mutually rewarding outcomes.

The techniques described in *A Stakeholder Approach to Issues Management* have proven effective in issues management projects around the world. They work equally well whether the stakeholders be illiterate subsistence villagers or internet savvy global activists. Corporate executives like the graphic, quantifiable tracking that the methods provide across time, regardless of the cultural locale. The techniques are especially apt for finding common ground and durable resolutions based on shared stakes in common concerns.

Keywords

Stakeholder networks, issues management, social issues, public issues, public affairs, corporate affairs, community relations, public relations, socio-political risk management, stakeholder engagement, corporate reputation, corporate social responsibility

Contents

Preface

Issue management is an inexact science; generally speaking, it concerns the assessment, analysis, and management of the inputs into managerial decision making, both strategic and tactical. There are even some who argue that some of the best outcomes are produced by approaching issues management as an intuitive art rather than a methodical science.[1] However, the view guiding this book is that issues management is an applied social science and therefore is subject to the same peculiarities as all other branches of the social sciences.

In the social sciences, the separation of the object of study and the perceiver doing the studying is incomplete to varying degrees. The overlap permits all sorts of biases on the perceiver's part to influence the description of the perceived. The problem is especially entrenched in politically charged areas of the social sciences such as issues management. Everyone has their political agenda whether they are aware of it or not, whether they admit it or not, and whether it makes a big difference or not. This not only makes it difficult for social scientists to escape the limitations that their biases put on their perceptions but also makes it difficult for practicing issues managers to resolve the controversies and conflicts that threaten to destroy whatever socially valuable institution or project they represent. Practitioners' biases can distort their views of the views of others and therefore limit their ability to predict the reactions of others.

As the field of issues management developed, techniques and perspectives were adapted from various social sciences to help deal with the fundamental challenges of being embedded in the very social system one is trying to understand and modify. Many techniques and practices developed in the mid-20th century assumed that natural science methods could be applied directly to the social sciences. We saw the rise of scientifically sampled public-opinion surveys and advertising practices applied to issues. In this so-called modern age, it was assumed that humankind and society could be perfected through the application of the principles of Western civilization's Enlightenment period.

Eventually it became clear that social systems react to expectations of them by evolving into different systems. Expecting ice to melt when exposed to heat does not change its behavior. Your expectations are irrelevant to what the ice will do. However, expecting political opposition to melt when exposed to political heat might stiffen the opposition's resolve—or not. Political opponents often react to each other's expectation of them. Because of people's capacity for reciprocal perspective taking, issues management techniques and principles (i.e., expectations) can quickly become invalid as soon as they become known. The social entities to whom the expectations apply (i.e., companies, communities, activist groups) change their behavior in response to the expectations of any perceivers who might prevent them from achieving their goals.

This phenomenon led to the late 20th-century popularity of the postmodern approach to issues management. Despairing of the possibility of a social science, the postmodern view portrayed social reality as being in a constant state of construction and invention. Applying that to the human activity of science itself and the culture that produced a false faith in science, postmodernism swung to the opposite extreme. It presumed that everything produced by Western civilization was unduly privileged and needed to be knocked off its pedestal. Therefore, the aim became to invent more and more issues rather than to resolve issues. However, issues managers have found some useful techniques from this source, too. For example, the postmodern assumption that all voices and perspectives are of equal value allows them to deflate the pretentions to moral superiority of those who campaign against their institutions or projects. More specifically, the postmodern technique of deconstructing messages for traces of stereotypes, gross generalizations, and self-serving biases allows issues managers to find the weak points in opponents' framing of issues.

The postmodern approach is also ultimately insufficient for practicing issues managers because it does not address their need to stand for something, as opposed to critiquing everything. In the end, issues managers have an institution or project to defend based on its valuable contribution to society. For this reason, most issues managers avoid taking sides in the cultural war between modern and postmodern approaches to social science and its applications. Instead, they look for whatever works. This book is intended to add a new set of tools to help just such eclectic issues managers.

CHAPTER 1

Why a Stakeholder Approach to Managing Issues?

Wal-Mart: A Company Whose Existence Became the Controversy

A stakeholder approach to managing issues works best when organized groups are championing the issues. Before we discuss the full meaning of "stakeholders" and "issues," let us look at a concrete example of an organization with stakeholder issues that it has to manage.

One of the most controversial organizations in the world is Wal-Mart. Wal-Mart is a private retailer based in the United States. It offers a wide range of merchandise and services, from clothing and food to pharmacy prescriptions and car tires. What makes it distinctive is the extent to which it has used the opportunities created by economic globalization to put the interest of customers and shareholders above all other interested parties (e.g., employees, unions, competitors, and suppliers). Those who benefit from Wal-Mart's strategy are dispersed and unorganized (i.e., retail customers, individual buyers of mutual fund units, and pension plan beneficiaries). Those who suffer from it are concentrated and organized at local levels (e.g., small retailers and unions). Moreover, as their numbers and visibility increase, they are increasingly capable of assisting one another as part of a global coalition of aggrieved Wal-Mart stakeholders.

The list of issues that has been brought against Wal-Mart includes the following:

- Abusing employee rights
- Violating child labor laws

- Failing to pay for hours worked
- Paying low wages
- Not providing adequate health benefits for employees
- Hiring illegal workers
- Promoting low wages in whole regions
- Causing the export of American jobs to Asia
- Exploiting foreign workers of suppliers
- Discriminating on the basis of gender
- Causing traffic congestion
- Destroying business districts in small towns
- Pricing merchandise predatorily
- Using public subsidies
- Driving suppliers into bankruptcy (i.e., monopolistic practices)
- Selling toxic products to children
- Degrading the environment and historic sites
- Symbolizing globalization

The charge of symbolizing globalization is particularly significant because it shows how much the company's reputation has suffered. This charge was made in a case where Wal-Mart bought a retail chain in Mexico known as Bodega Aurrera and built a store bearing that name in the low-income town of Teotihuacan, Mexico. Most of the town is visible from the nearby Pyramid of the Sun, a historic tourist attraction. However, the view of the town includes a view of the Bodega Aurrera store, and this therefore angered activists. They staged a hunger strike, claiming that the store was an offensive symbol of globalization. Meanwhile, on the opening day, hundreds of townspeople waited most of the day to shop in the store. The *San Diego Union Tribune* quoted one protester, Homero Aridjis, a Mexican novelist and poet, as saying, "We know that Teotihuacan isn't the most virgin of places in terms of construction and commerce . . . but Wal-Mart is a symbol . . . It's like nailing globalization's stake in the heart of old Mexico."[1] In other words, it was not the building that was the problem but rather the identity of the building's owner. Wal-Mart was accused of being Wal-Mart.

Wal-Mart's stunning status as a lightning rod for discontent can teach us a lesson about hidden factors that affect issues management.

The Network Asymmetry Behind the Controversy

The Wal-Mart case illustrates the benefits of a stakeholder approach to issues management. It shows how the dispersion or concentration of economic winners and losers is a significant determinant of controversy and affects strategies for managing the issues. Wal-Mart brings a global reach to the local retail environment. On the surface, it looks like a simple supplier–customer mediation strategy. Through low prices, they aggregate enough customers to replace profit from markups with profit from volume sales. But as experience shows, there are other impacted parties who join the game.

Originally, Wal-Mart's critics were local and concentrated. They were the economic losers in the competitive marketplace at the local level. At the same time, the economic winners (i.e., suppliers and customers) were dispersed geographically and unorganized. It was only Wal-Mart as the intermediary who worked at a global level.

With the help of journalists, activists, and unions, critics eventually formed broader and broader networks among themselves. In 1999, the book *Slam-Dunking Wal-Mart*, by Al Norman, ignited the anti-Wal-Mart movement. In 2004, Norman followed up with *The Case Against Wal-Mart*, which expanded the critique from Wal-Mart's impacts on communities to global supply chain issues and impacts.[2] The website WalMartSucks.org celebrated its 11th anniversary in 2011.[3] It specializes in horror stories from different countries about Wal-Mart's labor practices.

In today's political environment, the global and the local are as interconnected as atoms of hydrogen and oxygen in water. This has two important implications for the practice of issues management. First, global issues manifest themselves in local disputes and vice versa. Even something as seemingly local as traffic congestion can become an element of an international campaign (e.g., carbon emissions). Second, the ease of forming international networks today means that the issues management tactic of dividing and conquering the stakeholders is increasingly risky and futile.

In Wal-Mart's case, every issue has a group or groups that have an impact or want to have an impact. They are the stakeholders. Trying to manage the issues without developing relationships with the groups and the people behind them is like trying to direct a movie by going online and changing the script without ever talking to the actors or crew. Relationships with the real persons playing the roles are essential. These people are called stakeholders. The concept of a stakeholder is central to the approach described in this book. Let us look at what a stakeholder is and is not.

What Is a Stakeholder?

Social Actor: Person, Group, or Organization

A stakeholder is someone who is either affected by a company or can have an effect on the company. Note that this includes people who are at risk of being affected by the company and those who are capable of affecting the company even though they might not yet have acted.[4]

Sometimes the affected party is not a person but rather a group or organization, such as a church congregation or a fishers' cooperative. For this reason, more formal definitions of a stakeholder often use the term "social actor." A social actor is any person, group, or organization that can speak with one voice. This is an important extension because it allows us to include as stakeholders all sorts of social and political actors who can affect the company. Therefore, this gives us the definition of a stakeholder as a *social actor* who is affected by the company, at risk of being affected by the company, or who can affect the company.

The Nature of the Stake

The definition of a stakeholder implicitly equates stakes with impacts. The impacts can be either received or delivered, and they can be either positive or negative. That means that a company's best customer is just as much a stakeholder as a criminal gang that empties the company's warehouse overnight. Some theorists would rather think of stakeholders as only those who contribute to the company's wealth-creating capacity and who stand to gain or lose according to how the company fares.[5]

The problem with defining stakeholders as those whose interests are aligned with the company's interests is that it leaves social actors, such as corporate competitors and anticapitalist activists, outside the stakeholder category. Although it is a useful distinction for some purposes, for issues management we need to include those who are intent on harming the corporation. Therefore, in this book I simply mention the nature of the stakes and otherwise use the term "stakeholder" for all who are affected by or who can affect the company.

The Debate to Include Nonhumans as Stakeholders

There have been proposals to broaden the definition of a stakeholder to nonhumans that are affected by a company. Some suggest that the natural environment should be considered a stakeholder. The natural environment can be affected by a company's activities and, through channels such as climate change, can have an effect upon the company. However, because stakeholders raise issues that always involve an ethical element (e.g., fairness and reciprocity), any entity that cannot accept a moral responsibility cannot be a true stakeholder. The natural environment cannot, for example, enter into an agreement to refrain from raining on a parade in return for a company's promise to reduce carbon emissions. Therefore, it lacks a crucial criterion of moral agency implied in the concept of a stakeholder.[6] Moreover, the inclusion of nonhumans as stakeholders makes the concept so broad that it no longer offers a framework for developing strategy and planning action. It becomes useless to issues managers.[7] Therefore, although impacts on the natural environment are often of primary concern in issues management, in this book the word "stakeholder" is reserved for humans and human organizations because nonhuman entities do not participate in the debates and politics around issues.

It is not necessary to classify nonhumans as stakeholders in order to take account of impacts on them. Consider the following anecdote from a stakeholder relations project that I once worked on in a developing country: Subsistence villagers claimed that the spirit of a sacred rock was disturbed when a Western company built a road on the right-of-way it had leased from them. The villagers treated the rock as a stakeholder. They saw it as an animate being and therefore as a social actor. If the rock was indeed a social actor, it seemed to only speak through the villagers—specifically, through the village council. The council mediated between the rock and the company and apparently had the ability to know how much money in compensation payments would calm the rock down. The company was able to deal with the situation by treating the village council as the stakeholder—and by treating the rock as a rock.

If the company had treated the rock as a stakeholder, it would have been compelled to attempt direct negotiations with the rock. This is an example of how stakeholder theory could become useless to managers and to anyone else with a genuine interest in resolving disputes. Therefore, although it is important to take account of impacts on nonhuman entities, the word "stakeholder" is used here to refer to people, groups of people, or organizations formed by people.

The Focal Organization in Which the Stake Is Held

A related question is, "Stake in what?" What is the focal entity that stakeholders have stakes in? If we allow that the focal organization affected or being affected can be any kind of organization, then the definition of a stakeholder can be broadened. Rather than restricting the focal organization to private-sector companies, we can allow that the focal organization might be an nongovernmental organization (NGO), a branch of government, or a quasi-independent institution such as a university, a regional economic development council, an airport authority, a central bank, or a United Nations agency.

We may also broaden the definition by making the focal organization something more specific or more general. On the more specific side, it might be a specific project or operation of the focal organization, such as a single well of an international petroleum company, a single detachment of a city police force, a single project of an infrastructure company, or a single research center of a university.

On the more general side, we can distinguish between focal organizations that have been intentionally constituted and those that emerged spontaneously out of the patterned interactions of social actors. The former might be an NGO or a government department. The latter might be an organization, such as a neighborhood, a market and its supply chain, or a resource-harvesting industry such as a fishery or a grazing commons. These are organizations in the same sense that an ecosystem is an organization. It is a set of interdependencies that produce predictable patterns of behavior among the social actors involved. They quite often involve some role specialization as well, analogous to niches in ecosystems. For example, a geographical community could be considered this kind of emergent organization.[8]

If the focal organization is an emergent organization, then the social actors participating in it can be considered its stakeholders. Therefore, villagers would be stakeholders in their village. All the shepherds sharing a grazing commons would be stakeholders in the network of commons users. All the residents drawing from a river, and dumping into it, would be stakeholders in the network of users of the river's watershed (i.e., drainage region).

This use of the term "stakeholder" is new, but it does have precedent in the organizational science literature. The term "problem domain" has been used for nearly 30 years to describe such emergent systems that contain issues of concern to their stakeholder members.[9] Organizational and management scholars have tended to portray these types of organizations as networks and emphasize their ability to come into existence and evolve spontaneously, without having been planned.[10]

Elements of this thinking have emerged in the stakeholder theory literature. The view of the focal organization as possibly an emergent, self-sustaining network contrasts with the corporate-centric view of the focal organization. In an emergent network–type of focal organization, stakeholders can be viewed as making multiple microcontracts with one another.[11] This perspective highlights how business is only one of many stakeholders in a shared-problem domain.[12] If we put the focus on the shared problem, then the corporation is not the center of all its stakeholders but rather one of many social actors who all have a stake in finding a solution to the problems.[13]

In these types of emergent problem domain networks, the stakes are real, but none of the social actors is focal in the sense of having the power to change the impact through its own actions alone. All the stakeholders collectively might have that power, but they would have to act in a coordinated way. This is often called a commons dilemma or a shared resource dilemma. In management, it is called a problem domain—or simply a "mess."[14]

One objection to defining an emergent organization as a focal organization might be that it is difficult to attribute responsibilities to it. For example, consider a lake polluted by the residents around it. The lake cannot be given a social responsibility akin to corporate social responsibility (CSR). The problem of the pollution in the lake cannot be given a responsibility either. Therefore, at first glance, it might appear that this reciprocity-derived normative aspect of the relationship between stakeholder and focal organization has been lost. Upon closer analysis, however, it becomes clear that the stakeholders are the residents and the focal organization is the network formed by their relations with one another. If there are no relationships, their individual responsibilities are to form relationships adequate to achieving the collaboration that would solve the shared problem. Therefore, when we define stakeholders by the stake they share in a problem domain, we are postulating the network among them as the focal organization. This begs the question about what characteristics the network should have to be effective at discharging the shared responsibilities of the stakeholders. This is an empirical research question. Chapter 3 presents some hypotheses about how various network structures imply specific kinds of barriers to a network becoming responsible and accountable.

Therefore, I adopt a broader definition of stakeholder to include the social actors who can affect or be affected by a focal organization, whether the organization is intentionally structured or emergent.

Stakeholder Relations and Business Ethics

Issues by their nature are political and involve value judgments. They usually entail claims about what is fair versus unfair, legitimate versus illegitimate, and ethical versus unethical. For this reason, those who try to apply stakeholder theory to the management of issues faced by corporations necessarily tread in the field of business ethics. However, that does not make stakeholder theory a guide to business ethics. There is enormous confusion on this point.

Stakeholder theory does say that focal organizations have responsibilities to their stakeholders. However, contrary to popular opinion, it does not say what those responsibilities might be.[15] In order to specify the nature of the responsibilities (e.g., which stakeholder's interests get higher priority), one must invoke ethical criteria appropriate to the situation at hand.

The confusion about stakeholder theory itself providing ethical guidance arose from rhetoric that contrasted stakeholder interests with stockholder interests. The ethical stance endorsed by economist Milton Friedman[16] was often identified as a stockholder-first approach to management priority setting. That was then contrasted with a stakeholder approach, which took account of a broader set of interested parties.[17] Then it would be typically argued that, for various ethical reasons, the stakeholder approach was morally superior.

The flaw in the stockholder–stakeholder contrast was that critics of Friedman's exhortation to put financiers' interests first had taken those arguments out of their historical and social context. At the time Friedman formulated this advice, business was mostly domestic. Globalization had not yet taken off. Moreover, Friedman was giving advice to mostly U.S.-based executives. The business environment in the preglobalization United States was populated by extremely powerful stakeholders (e.g., unions and business associations) who had joined with government in devising a system for insuring that the wealth of large corporations would be shared broadly with the rest of society. Robert Reich, a former U.S. secretary of labor, describes mid-20th-century capitalism in the United States as a system of interlocking institutions that effectively harnessed the wealth creation of corporations to create an enormous affluent middle class.[18] Therefore, Friedman's advice was given to executives who were *forced* to share the benefits with stakeholders. According to Reich's description of the demands on mid-20th-century U.S. executives, their time was mostly taken up with mandatory, institutionalized negotiations with stakeholders. Therefore, Friedman probably saw many executives being completely absorbed by these social responsibilities and therefore offered them an ethic to rebalance their priorities.

Critics of Friedman's ethical stance are actually criticizing the continued use of that advice in a world where globalization, according to Reich, has dismantled the institutions that bound corporations in the broadly consensual social contract of an earlier era. That is fair criticism in itself. However, most of the critics fail to acknowledge that Friedman's advice was socially responsible in its historical context. By that failure, they become vulnerable to thinking that the new stakeholder approach somehow includes an element of social responsibility not included in earlier approaches to management.

Edward Freeman, the father of stakeholder theory, called this kind of thinking the separation fallacy, which means one can make purely business decisions devoid of any ethical choice.[19] Once the fallacy has been accepted, it then makes sense to try to integrate ethics with business. In the approach taken in this book, we agree with Freeman that no integration is necessary. It makes as much sense as trying to integrate two sides of a coin.

Ethics is an unavoidable part of business decision making, and business is an unavoidable part of ethical decision making. The interdependence of the two is particularly evident in the field of issues management. Issues management in a globalized business environment continually confronts us with decisions that affect the kind of global social contract that will or will not evolve as interests of diverse stakeholders vie for recognition, support, and even dominance. These decisions always involve an element of ethics. A stakeholder approach to issues management helps identify those elements but does not in itself provide ethical guidance.

The Fit Among Ethical Frameworks and Approaches to Issues Management

Some views of stakeholders and their issues are easier to integrate than others with particular approaches to business ethics. For example, a definition that leaves antagonistic, anticorporate social actors outside the stakeholder category is more suitable if one focuses primarily on an ethical approach to issues management involving some level of dialogue or stakeholder engagement.[20] Dialogue as an approach to ethical decision making was central in the early work[21] of social philosopher Jürgen Habermas.

To simplify, Habermas said that ethical decisions would emerge when everyone can talk it over as equals without any intimidation or power differentials. Obviously, leaving competitors and enemies out of the talks would make this approach a lot more feasible. Defining them as nonstakeholders makes it easier in practice to ignore them or treat them with a completely different policy. That reserves the dialogue or engagement policies for more reasonable social actors.

Habermas himself agreed that trying to create an ideal speech situation is not very practical.[22] That is why he revised his ethical framework.

In his later work, he says that democratic societies come close enough to the ideal speech situation that they can legitimize and delegitimize whatever patterns of stakeholder relations they deem ethical or unethical. This view has the advantage of allowing issues managers to deem all social actors as stakeholders if they affect the issue or are affected by it, whether positively or negatively. Moreover, this view acknowledges that political battles are infused with questions of fairness, justice, and justification. Such ethical questions are often decisive in winning political support for a position in the whole struggle over how any sector (e.g., business or NGOs) or industry (e.g., energy) should be regulated. Winning a political contest involves many different ethics-laden decisions such as those that arise in developing a network of trusting relations, weaving together alliances that legitimately represent the interests of diverse stakeholders, and leading in the direction of responsible change.[23] Thus, in this view, although even crooks can be stakeholders, ethical questions appear at the center of the issues manager's work exactly because it is political work conducted in a democratic context.

An increasingly serious disadvantage of relying of democratic political contexts to justify the outcomes of controversies is that it provides no guidance for dealing with stakeholder organizations from undemocratic societies.[24] Because their whole society fails to meet the conditions for fair decision making, the morality of the relations established by organizations from such a society cannot be determined. This is cold comfort for a manager negotiating a price with a corporation owned by a dictatorial state that imprisons foreigners for reasons that are not made public. It is one thing to allow that unethical actors can sometimes be stakeholders; it is quite another to operate in a system where actors of questionable ethics set the rules for the conduct of business.

In his 2003 book, *Stakeholder Theory and Organizational Ethics*, Robert Phillips[25] applied the moral philosophy of John Rawls to the stakeholder relations field. Under this system, issues managers would put themselves in the shoes of the most disadvantaged stakeholder and decide what would be fair if there were a chance they might find themselves stuck in those shoes. In this approach, a corporation is behaving ethically to the extent that it supports a set of rules of conduct that grants concessions to underdogs.

The unarticulated master discourse inspiring the application of Rawlsian criteria is that corporations are powerful and stakeholders are intimidated or otherwise bullied. Phillips's contribution is useful to the extent that this is true. However, it does not provide ethical guidance to organizations facing a powerful coalition of organizations intent on delegitimizing it, robbing it, or putting it out of existence. Likewise, the integrative social contracts theory[26] does not seem to work when the focal organization itself is the target of intimidation and bullying. In most of what has been written at the interface between stakeholder theory and business ethics, it is always the corporation that needs ethical guidance—never the stakeholders.[27] Criminal organizations, dictators, extortion groups, "not in my backyard"[28] groups, and other assorted rent seekers and free riders are seldom even mentioned as stakeholders, let alone studied as the dominant rule makers. Nonetheless, globalization is making their power in many jurisdictions an increasingly urgent and perplexing problem.

Informed Eclecticism

It is not the intent of this book to present an ethical foundation for business decisions or a business foundation for ethical decisions. We have acknowledged that issues management, like all areas of business decision making, necessarily entails ethical decisions. We have briefly surveyed a few of the major approaches to ethical decision making. From this it is obvious that they each have their merit, but none is perfect for all applications and circumstances. Therefore, in this book we take a stance of informed ethical eclecticism, always striving to articulate the ethical aspects of the choices we encounter as we strive to improve the practice of issues management.

The view of stakeholders taken in the approach described here treats all social actors as having both business and ethical concerns. In this view, social actors who are unethical can be found among focal organizations and their stakeholders alike. The refusal to view stakeholders implicitly as less powerful but more legitimate social actors allows us to extend the stakeholder approach to applications beyond the global corporation from a democratic society.

By maintaining a stance of informed ethical eclecticism, we can easily apply the stakeholder approach to new arenas, such as to small entrepreneurial start-ups facing established stakeholders with vested interests, to companies operating in places where the rule of law is thin, or to companies facing mutually shared problems requiring governance regimes that do not yet exist.

The Remaining Chapters

The remainder of the book unfolds as follows. In chapter 2, you will learn where issues come from, with particular emphasis on the role of stakeholder networks as the conveyor of issue legitimacy. In chapter 3, we look at a tool kit of nine patterns of social capital in stakeholder networks that can be used to diagnose the sociopolitical dynamics that will be encountered in trying to manage issues raised by stakeholders. Chapter 4 describes practical techniques for collecting information on issues and the stakeholders who are concerned about them. Then in chapter 5, you will learn how to summarize the information in ways that remove the noise and bring the main themes forward. For example, we look at how to graph the links among issues in the minds of different groupings of stakeholders. Chapter 6 guides you through techniques for combining such clarified information in ways that suggest strategies for issues management. Finally, in chapter 7 we turn to the question of winning support for a stakeholder network approach to issues management inside your organization and the more fundamental question of the contribution of this approach to resolving global issues in a world without a legitimate global authority.

Questions for Managers

The ideas in this chapter can be applied to the issues management challenges of most organizations. Here are some questions to prompt insights about their applicability to your situation:

- Which stakeholders are affected by your organization's activities? Which can affect your organization's activities? Which are in both categories?

- What issues are out of your direct control and yet affect your organization? What issues are beyond your direct control and yet could be influenced, for better or worse, by your organization's activities?
- Who are the stakeholders in the problems or issues that are beyond your direct control but that affect you or can be affected by you?
- Which of your stakeholders appear to be dispersed or disorganized now? Are they net beneficiaries of your organization's activities? What would be the advantages or disadvantages of more coherent articulation of their support or criticism?

CHAPTER 2

Where Do Issues Come From?

The Consequences of Controversies

Resource Access for Competitive Advantage

Controversies have negative impacts on organizations when they reduce access to resources. Organizations need access to resources such as raw materials, premises, employees, financing, suppliers, and customers. Those companies that succeed in securing superior access to valuable, scarce, nonsubstitutable resources gain a competitive advantage over others.[1]

Access to resources can be controlled directly by a wide variety of stakeholders, including municipalities, government licensing bodies, industry regulators, unions, banks, stock exchanges, and other financial intermediaries. Access can also be directly or indirectly influenced by community groups, citizens' organizations, environmental groups, competitors, industry organizations, professional associations, and innovators (e.g., in research institutes or in private companies). Most of these stakeholder categories can include players that operate at the international or national levels and not just at the level of local operational sites. Therefore, getting access to resources is more than just a matter of developing a favorable relationship with one resource gatekeeper; it is a matter of building a sociopolitical coalition that has legitimacy in the stakeholder network.[2]

The phenomenon of losing access to resources necessary to an organization's competitive position is not all or none. An organization can experience problems that make resource access more expensive but not impossible. Reduced access can range in severity from minimal to complete. The ability of stakeholders to alter the degree of access is called the social license to operate (SLO), or simply the social license. It is usually expressed in terms of the degree of risk of reduced access. An organization that has full access and very low risk of reduced access in the future has a full social license. Table 2.1 shows some examples of stakeholder networks that have either reduced or completely blocked a company's access to essential resources.

The top row of Table 2.1 deals with the retail sector. In the United States and Canada, Wal-Mart often faces opposition to its plans for new store locations. The opponents have gone from being independent local coalitions of labor unions and merchants' associations to being linked nationally through full-time anti-Wal-Mart activists. Some of these activists are journalistic entrepreneurs, such as the author Al Norman, while others are unions.[3] They cannot stop Wal-Mart directly. Their usual tactic is to pressure local municipalities into rejecting Wal-Mart's development application. In other words, because of losing its SLO, Wal-Mart is prevented from obtaining a legal license. Of course, Wal-Mart can always find another site in a friendlier jurisdiction. However, this restriction on its resource access yields opportunities to its several competitors.

Table 2.1. Examples of Stakeholder Networks That Control Resource Access

Focal organization	Resource	Resource-controlling stakeholder	Stakeholders influencing controlling stakeholder
Wal-Mart	Local building sites for stores	Municipal council	Coalition of local merchants, labor union activists, and sometimes environmentalists
Tata Motors	Building site for factory in India	Local farmers unhappy with the price received for their land	Other farmers in other regions willing to sell for prices that make moving the plant economical
Monterrico Metals	Copper deposit at Rio Blanco, one of the richest in the world	Local council (via social license)	None with enough power

The second row in Table 2.1 deals with the manufacturing sector. In January 2008, Tata Motors made headlines with the announcement of its plan to manufacture the Nano, the world's lowest cost automobile with an anticipated selling price of US$2,500. Based in India, Tata acquired 1,000 acres of land for a manufacturing plant near Singur, West Bengal. The state appropriated the land from poor farmers and offered them very low compensation. After Tata had built a $350 million manufacturing plant on 600 acres, the farmers blocked the freeway beside the plant and demanded a better compensation package. Tata refused and threatened to abandon the plant on that site and search for an alternative location to build a second plant. In September 2008, the Singur farmers accepted a compensation package involving the return of 400 acres and the purchase of outside land to replace the 600 acres already used. Production went ahead at the Singur site. However, when the Nano came to market in 2009, it was priced at US$3,000 in Delhi.[4]

Tata lost its SLO and therefore could not exercise the legal license it already had. Even though it could have substituted the resource (i.e., the Singur land) with an alternative resource (i.e., land elsewhere), the cost of doing so would have ruined its plans to sell the Nano for US$2,500. Even the compromise that was reached caused the Nano to come to market at a less competitive price.

The third row in Table 2.1 shows an example from the natural resources sector. Monterrico Metals is a UK-based mineral exploration company that until recently was listed on the alternative investment market of the London stock exchange. It announced drilling results in 2003 indicating that the exploration site known as a Rio Blanco might be among the top five copper deposits in the world. There was also evidence of some molybdenum. During 2004, share prices rose from around 150p to 600p. In early 2005, Monterrico was touting late 2007 as a possible date for production to begin.

From 2004 to 2007, local villagers and farmers marched in protest against mining in the area, making it clear that they did not grant a social license to the project. In February of 2007, 90% of Monterrico Metals was purchased by a consortium led by Zijin, a Chinese mining company, at a price of 340 pence per share. However, the protests continued. In May 2007, six more people were injured in a protest to stop all mining in the region. In September 2007, a referendum showed strong community opposition to the project. Instead of starting production in late 2007, Monterrico ended the year with a stalled project. Nonetheless, they persisted.

In 2008, photographs were released showing that in 2005 protesters had been tortured in the Rio Blanco camp. Two were shot and one was killed. Charges were brought against the company, its security subcontractor, and the police. By March 2009, the investigation concluded that the police were responsible for the torture. It absolved Monterrico, its parent company Zijin, and its security subcontractor. However, the violence continued. In November 2009, two or three Monterrico employees lost their lives when the mining camp was attacked by 15 to 20 opponents.[5] In June 2009, Zijin delisted Monterrico in an attempt to cut costs. By then the share price had risen back up to around 100p after falling as low as 23p. At delisting, investors who bought in late 2004 lost about 80% of their investment, mostly because the project never had a social license.[6]

The Monterrico case is a complex ongoing conflict involving allegations of wrongdoing on all sides. Reports filled with inflammatory language and designed to further political ends obscure the actual events. Chains of command for several of the parties involved stretch from the remote villages around the Rio Blanco site to the faraway capitals of Lima, London, and Beijing. It is difficult to discern who is responsible for actions taken along various links in these chains. One thing is clear: Behind the conflict, there is a power struggle between the local communities and some part of the national government of Peru. It amounts to a contest between the legal license issued by the government and the social license withheld by the communities.

Social License to Operate

As Table 2.1 shows, stakeholders and stakeholder coalitions often only succeed in reducing a company's access to resources without completely blocking access. This gradation is expressed more formally in the concept of the SLO. Ian Thomson, a community relations consultant in the mining industry, and I developed the first formal theoretical statement of what is meant by the SLO.[7] At its core the SLO is the level of acceptance or rejection accorded to a project by its stakeholder network. It is distinct from a legal license in that the power of the stakeholders has not been institutionalized. They can enforce their decisions just as effectively as issuers of legal licenses can, but they rely more on legitimacy in a network than on institutionalized legitimacy. Therefore, it is a license only in a metaphorical sense.

An SLO is typically withdrawn by blocking access to resources. For example, a boycott might block a company's access to markets and customers. A strike blocks access to labor. A road blockade might block a company's access to a plant or other physical resource location. These are examples of the loss of the SLO through direct blockage of access. Quite often, those who withdraw the SLO form alliances with other stakeholders who have the power to issue legal licenses. For example, a citizens group opposing a development might convince city councilors that their political future depends on withholding a legal license for the project.

The term "social license to operate" was coined by James Cooney in 1997, then an executive at Placer Dome Inc., a gold-mining company that no longer exists. In a meeting with the World Bank, he used the term to describe the sociopolitical challenges facing the mining industry at the time. World Bank officials then began using the term, and it spread throughout the mining industry. Now it is common parlance in wider management circles.[8] Most authors who have written about the SLO emphasize that it can fluctuate across time and therefore needs to be constantly maintained. It is not a one-time checklist item that can be earned and then set aside as an achievement.

Ian Thomson and I hypothesized four levels of the SLO (see Figure 2.1). The lowest is a withheld or withdrawn SLO. At this level, the licensing stakeholder or stakeholders have no trust in the company, do not see it as credible, and question its legitimacy. The next level is called acceptance because the company is seen as legitimate, but the stakeholders still doubt its credibility and do not trust it. They take a wait-and-see attitude while allowing the project to proceed. This is the level at which most projects begin. The third level is called approval. At this level, the focal organization is seen as both legitimate and credible but has not yet earned full trust. Stakeholders actively support the project. This is highest level most companies ever achieve. The fourth level is called identification because the stakeholders come to identify psychologically with the project or the industry. This only occurs when full trust is achieved. Examples include communities that identify with their leading industries, such as

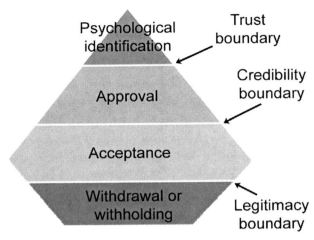

Figure 2.1. Levels of SLO.

Hollywood with the film industry and Silicon Valley with the computer industry.

Controversy and Reputation

An organization's reputation can affect its access to resources. Positive corporate performances can enhance a company's reputation and facilitate resource access. A negative reputation can reduce resource access and therefore decrease the organization's chances of survival. Although most organizations benefit from a good reputation, some benefit from a bad reputation. Mexican drug cartels, for example, probably incur lower enforcement costs when their reputation as good corporate citizens declines. For most organizations, however, controversy creates a risk of damage to their reputation with the subsequent risk of reduced resource access. However, that is not the only possible outcome. Sometimes a controversy will only polarize sentiments for and against an organization. The organization's supporters might become even more supportive.

Figure 2.2 shows the relationships among what an organization does, the development controversy, effects on the organization's reputation, and subsequent effects on the organization's access to resources. When an organization's performance is taken for granted, there is no controversy

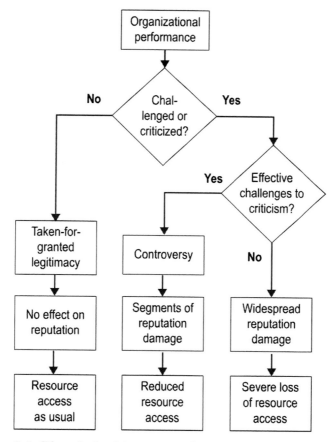

Figure 2.2. The relationships among what an organization does, the development of controversy, effects on reputation, and access to resources.

and no effect on the organization's access to resources. Controversy occurs when the organization's performance is questioned, challenged, or criticized by someone in public but not everyone agrees with the criticism.

What makes reputation distinctive is the lack of direct network ties. It is more of a mass media phenomenon. The stakeholder model applies at the stage of managing the impact of the controversy. When reputation is in the eyes of those who have direct ties to the organization, it is part of the relationship. When it is in the eyes of unorganized members of mass stakeholder groups, it risks becoming a cultural assumption. People start to act in unison without the need for organization and network norms. It becomes a cultural norm and, as such, drives spontaneous individual behavior. At that point, the stakeholder approach is less effective by itself and should be supplemented with a public opinion change approach.

Issue Life Cycle Models in the National Context

The Domestic Issue Paradigm

Issues develop through stages. There are many models of issue life cycles. They typically depict the final stage or stages of the issue life cycle as involving some sort of action by government. The version in Figure 2.3 is a compilation of existing models into a composite that includes the most common features of all life cycle models.[9]

When the Blame Story Is Developed

In the issue life cycle model in Figure 2.3, the earlier a company identifies and acts on the issue, the more influence the company can have. In the later stages, management discretion is reduced to damage control and regulatory compliance. Phase 1 is a period when small groups of people share their complaints among themselves. As they discuss their dissatisfaction, their expectations and analysis of the situation becomes more articulated. In a process known as framing,[10] they develop a version of

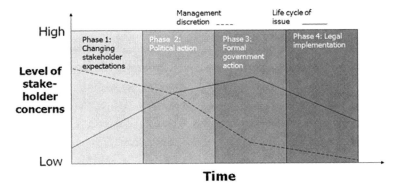

Figure 2.3. Typical issue life cycle model to date.

events that describes the injustice of the current situation and legitimizes opposition to it. This becomes a collective action frame (CAF). The CAF includes answers to questions about the nature of the negative consequences suffered, who is to blame, and what should be done.[11] In plain language, the initial stakeholders develop a blame story. They often also create a shared identity, or victim identity, that facilitates the organization of public protests and justifies demands for changes.

When the Issue Becomes Public

Public protest and media communications are highlighted in phase 2. The stakeholders with the complaints begin a grassroots campaign and therefore become classifiable as a social movement. The social movement aims to garner political support for the frame that has been developed for the issue. In earlier times this stage typically involved protest rallies and marches. This requires a great deal of network building. Today, social media have facilitated the networking. New tactics are appearing, such as flash protests (i.e., organized by cell phone and website coordination) and communications via all the Internet-supported social media.

If enough people absorb the social movement's framing of the issue, their numbers represent a threat and an opportunity for government officials. If the government ignores the demands of a growing and vocal segment of the public, it risks being seen as unresponsive and therefore unsuited for office. If, however, it adapts the frame, it risks alienating those who resist the frame. On the opportunity side, if those being alienated do not have as much political clout as those in the social movement, then the government can win popularity by being responsive. Because the costs and benefits are usually not clear to politicians at this point, the typical response is some manner of study or inquiry. These exercises are ostensibly designed to sort out the truth from the propaganda in the social movement's framing of the issue. In reality, they are exercises in exploring the possible points of compatibility between public opinion and the existing legal framework. If public opinion is hardening against the social movement's framing of the issue, the issue will stall at this stage. Likewise, if accepting the social movement's frame would require a significant overhaul of the legal system, it is not likely to move to the next stage. However, this is rare. Stakeholders usually take this into account when they create the frame. In most cases, the inquiry exercise ends up granting at least some measure of legitimacy to the social movement's framing of the issue.

The final stage is government regulation and/or legislation. At this point new rules are created and implemented. Hereafter, the focal organization has very little influence on the course of the issue. The framing has been settled and the remaining questions are technical matters related to administration of the new rules. Broad public interest in the issue begins to fade as the matter transitions from grassroots campaigning to bureaucratic committee work.

Issue Life Cycles in the Postnational Context

Questioning Assumptions About the Rule of Law

Issue life cycle models always presume a sociopolitical context. Usually the context is an implicit assumption shared by the author and the reader. The models previously described implicitly assume (a) an effective government that (b) permits popular movements and (c) responds to them. Those models are good guides for controversies that mostly involve domestic companies in democracies of the developed world. The fatal flaw that limits the generality of existing life cycle models is the presumption of the rule of law. There are three geopolitical levels where the rule of law turns out to be a faulty assumption.

At the first, most global level, corporate horizons have expanded beyond the rule of domestic laws. Transnational corporations now face a range of controversies that no one political jurisdiction can settle with its own regulatory regime. National governments have had variable success at creating effective global regulations for business. For example, there is no international government to standardize labor and environmental regulations among the nations of Asia, Latin America, Africa, and North America. Global crime networks have come to threaten the rule of law in several international regions. Like a virus, global terrorism morphs continually. Despite an unprecedented effort to curb global carbon emissions, hope is dim for effective, concerted action. While we wait for the next pandemic to sweep the planet, the lack of global financial regulation has reduced the ability of all actors to contribute to solutions to any of these problems.

At the national level, more of the world's internationally active corporations are now owned by nation-states. In these cases, the regulator and the regulated are one. Moreover, some of the most significant state corporations are owned by dictatorships and monarchies. For example, 88% of the world's proven oil reserves in 2007 were controlled by state-owned oil companies.[12] This means that framing and mobilizing stages of typical issue life cycle models would see citizens campaigning against an arm of the state. Some states do not permit the mobilization of protest against any of its arms. Even if a campaign were permitted and successful, the later stages of existing models would see the state (a) admitting to wrongdoing and (b) punishing itself. Notice how the rising economic clout of corporations owned by dictatorships reveals the cultural embeddedness of current issue life cycle models. The rule of law might seem heavy in a dictatorship, but where the state regulates itself, it is less the rule of law and more the rule of might.

At the local level, there has been a shift from national independence movements to community autonomy movements. Disaffected communities around the world now shun the goal of nationhood. They see how globalization is weakening the institution of the nation-state. It no longer looks like such an attractive road to autonomy. Instead, today's insurgents seek self-governance inside the national state. They no longer want all the onerous responsibilities of nationhood. However, they demand the right to veto anything that affects them, particularly anything related to land or resource use. When Peru signed a free trade agreement with the United States in 2009 it pretended to have sovereignty over an indigenous area of the Amazon region. The battle at the Devil's Curve proved otherwise: When the national government attempted to assert its sovereignty, 11 police were killed and 38 were taken hostage.[13] Now companies wanting to extract gas from the region have to deal with indigenous authorities, as well as the national government in Lima. Likewise, when Douglas Creek Estates purchased land from the municipality of Caledonia, Ontario, it falsely believed that Canadian law would protect its property rights. Nearby indigenous "warriors" occupied the land, claiming that the 1844 sale of the land by their ancestors was not valid. Instead of protecting property rights, the police investigated those who objected to the warriors' armed intimidation of townspeople. Nearly a decade after the dispute began, supporters of the warriors block other construction sites and demand taxes from legal property owners. Repeated court orders to halt such activity are simply ignored because an ever-expanding category of residents realizes that they have successfully exempted themselves from the full rule of law.[14]

These examples show how issues management theories must be updated to apply to a wider variety of sociopolitical situations. The models of issue life cycles that include final stages involving legislation or regulation apply to a declining proportion of circumstances in today's global business environment. As more business is being conducted where the rule of law is thin, approaches to issues management that rely on legal knowledge and legislative lobbying become less universally applicable. What kind of models would match today's realities?

Three Basic Forms of Governance

Today companies find themselves operating under all sorts of governance—not just governance by government. Governance is different from government in that government is only one possible provider of governance. Sociologists and political scientists have identified three classic sources of governance:[15]

1. Hierarchies (governments and formal organizations)
2. Markets
3. Networks

Hierarchies are typically used when transactions require more specific knowledge, equipment, and coordination. Hierarchies legitimize their governance through employment relationships and contracts. Communication among the actors takes place according to prescribed processing routines. For example, putting together an automobile requires specific knowledge, equipment, and coordination. Some people do build their own cars by buying the parts here and there in the open market, but if everyone had to do that, traffic congestion would disappear.

Markets are used more when transactions do not require any specific knowledge, materials, or coordination. Property rights legitimize market governance, and the actors send signals via prices (i.e., offers, bids, and settlements). Buying gasoline is a pure market transaction. No special knowledge or equipment is required to switch from one gas station to another.

Networks are used more when there is high uncertainty about how to evaluate what is being exchanged. Networks are especially preferred for transactions involving intangibles and questions of reputation. Network governance is legitimized by the norm of reciprocity. The parties enter into a transaction voluntarily and expect mutual benefits, at least over the longer term, and at least from other members of the network—if not from the specific member being dealt with at any moment. This is a generalized expectation of reciprocity. Buying a used car, for example, is often a high-uncertainty transaction. It may be a stereotype, but used-car dealers do not enjoy a sterling reputation. Unless one is a mechanic, it is difficult to evaluate the value of what is offered. For that reason, people often buy used cars through networks of trusted family members and friends.

Sometimes these sources of governance come into conflict. As a case in point, a power struggle arose between a market and a hierarchy in late 2010 when Ireland was about to receive European Union (EU) assistance to bolster its banking system. The markets began to drive down the value of the euro. EU government leaders strove to prop it up.[16] In countries where the official currency exchange rate (i.e., controlled by government hierarchy) is at odds with market demand (i.e., the price buyers are willing to pay in the market), the network form of governance is used to circumvent the hierarchical form. Networks of trusted contacts form to facilitate transactions in black markets.

When both markets and hierarchies do not provide governance, the default provider is the network.[17] For example, in preliterate societies where the closest thing to a hierarchy is a council of elders, and the closest thing to a market is barter with neighboring tribes, the norms of the group are enforced by the threat of ostracism from the social network. The network members acting in concert provide the governance.

Issue Management as the Struggle for Legitimacy

The network form of governance is becoming more important as more of a corporation's issues arise in contexts where the rule of law is thin. The ultimate utilitarian aim of issues management is to maintain solid access to the essential resources that make the firm competitive. This amounts to having that access accepted as routine and taken for granted. In technical terms, this level of acceptance is a type of legitimacy.[18] It is particularly essential that the access-controlling stakeholders see the firm's resource access as uncontestable.

Issue campaigns are attempts to delegitimize a company's access to resources. In the past, issues were resolved when the government stepped in and changed the rules and conditions for the resource access. Through formal legal regulations, government legitimized a new taken-for-granted routine for resource access. How can issues ever be resolved when there is no government to step in and relegitimize the resource access?

The problem of maintaining legitimacy when the legitimacy provided by government hierarchy is thin also arises in the related field of corporate social responsibility (CSR). Issues management and CSR are related insofar as all the supposed social responsibilities of corporations either are or have been issues. For example, the criteria used by ethical investment funds to screen companies on their performance of their social responsibilities reads like a list of current and past issues. They include environmental criteria (e.g., carbon footprint, pollution, health impacts, and biodiversity impacts), labor relations (e.g., working conditions and employee safety), employment equity (e.g., in terms of gender, sexuality, and race), supplier treatment (e.g., child labor and fair trade), community stakeholder treatment (e.g., human rights abuse, disputes, engagement, and consultation), social impacts (e.g., arms used in crime and warfare, addictive products, and pornography), and positive criteria such as community development or investment (e.g., poverty and social inequality).

If CSR is to perform the function of legitimizing the role of business in today's globalized economy, it must find a basis for legitimacy even where the rule of law and liberal democracy does not exist. There is no legitimacy globally because there is no global government. There is no legitimacy in dictatorships and oligarchies because there is no democracy. In autonomous subnational regions, legitimacy is disputed. Locals successfully challenge the legitimacy of the nation-state. So what is a firm to do in order to find a legitimized solution to an issue? One possible option is a form of stakeholder democracy.[19]

In the context of issues management, stakeholder democracy would imply that solid access to resources has to be founded on legitimacy gained through a decision-making forum voluntarily authorized by its participants. It would be more than engaging in dialogue with stakeholders insofar as it leads to joint decision making, mutually assented accords, and eventually, new decision-making institutions to provide governance. This kind of legitimization doesn't come from a national government and cannot be bought through philanthropy or liberal, democratic-style CSR. It can only be created by a network. It is legitimacy achieved through the network form of governance.

Achieving Legitimacy in Network Governance Regimes

Increasingly, issues management is about keeping resource access through achieving legitimization of that access in a network of stakeholders capable of collaborating to create and enforce network norms. This is not some utopian goal for the distant future. Without all the fancy theorizing about legitimacy or liberal democratic assumptions, companies are coming to this view through a trial-and-error process of practical problem solving. By simply pursuing what works, this is where they end up.

There are a number of these governance networks at the global level. They are called global action networks. The Forestry Stewardship Council (FSC) is an example. It is an international association of forest owners, timber industry associations, academics, social groups, and environmental organizations. They meet to share information and search for better forest management practices. The FSC also certifies forest products that meet certain standards of forest management and conservation. Because of the scale and diverse complexity, however, the global level might be the most difficult level at which to create effective governance networks. There are many more successful examples at the national and local levels.[20] Generally, attempts to create legitimacy-conferring networks are more successful when they involve a wide diversity of stakeholders in the problem or issue, and they allow time and occasion for the development of mutual understanding and trust among the participants.

Issue Life Cycles Under Network Governance Regimes

If we return to the question of issue life cycles with a broader perspective on what governance and legitimization means, then it appears that the model in Figure 2.3 would have to be modified to look more like Figure 2.4. Notice that the first two stages are the same, but the last two have been changed into an ongoing involvement with the network of stakeholders. This reiterates the point made in connection with the SLO—namely, that it is an ongoing process of maintaining legitimacy and increasing credibility and trust. The figure shows the level of stakeholder concern declining on the right-hand side on the assumption that the level of SLO rises with ongoing participation in the network. The third phase is part of an ongoing process that ranges from reestablishing legitimacy to gaining credibility and, eventually, trust. For this reason, managerial discretion stays relatively moderate instead of declining as it does in the domestic national life cycle (Figure 2.3).

Influencing the Influential

Both of the issue life cycle models (Figure 2.3 and 2.4) imply that the number of people and organizations involved in the issue grows steadily over time. In the beginning, the issue is known and discussed in relatively small circles. There may be only one organization concerned about it.

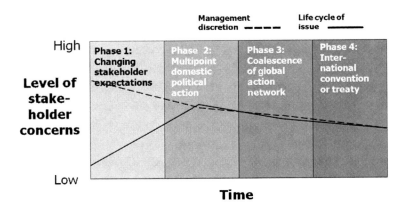

Figure 2.4. Issue life cycle model for circumstances where network governance prevails.

In the final stages, two changes occur. First, to the extent that the issue campaigning is successful, masses of mutually unconnected people may become aware of the issue. Second, as some form of governance comes to take account of the issue, additional organizations become involved. Under the rule of law, these tend to be government agencies. Where the rule of law is thin, they are more likely to be other stakeholders in the issue. This has implications for the communications and management strategies.

In the early stages, stakeholder network approaches work best. In the later stages, the strategy must be more differentiated. Stakeholder network approaches continue to work best in dealing with governance bodies, however, mass marketing and public opinion approaches can also become useful in for dealing with the reputational effects and for reframing.

Public Opinion Approach

The public opinion approach to issues management consists of communications aimed at changing the perceptions of masses of individuals. The typical tools include media coverage, press releases, and advertising. The stakeholder network approach and the public opinion approach are often complementary. The former concentrates on opinions and political support as mobilized in groups. The latter concentrates on mass individual opinion and behavior.

There tend to be two main strategies that call for the public opinion approach. First, when the members of the mass audience control resource access directly, the strategy is to affect their individual behavior directly. This is the case, for example, when the company sells a branded product at the retail level. The consumers directly control the company's access to revenues. Cigarette companies suffered this fate in several states when the U.S. government–sponsored social-marketing campaigns changed public attitudes toward smoking. Demand for cigarettes declined as a result of individual decisions taken by masses of people.[21]

Second, the public opinion approach is useful when the members of the mass audience do not control resource access directly but influence those who do. This can occur, for example, when the mass audience doubles as an electorate in a democracy. They can pressure the government to regulate or terminate the company's access to any input materials, process requirements, or markets. For example, mass media campaigns in Europe created voter opposition to baby seal fur from Canada. As a result of this public opinion, the EU banned the import of baby seal pelts. This dynamic also occurs when consumers shun products that do not bear a particular certification (e.g., green or safe). In those cases, mass consumers pressure large retailers to change their offerings, which causes restricted market access for the company.

Changing mass opinion requires a combination of analysis and creativity. Analytic tools such as public opinion surveys and focus groups are the mainstay of this approach. There are hundreds of books on how to use these tools. Moreover, social psychologists have written volumes on the factors that influence opinion change. Crafting the right combination of message and medium takes some creativity. Public opinion surveys cannot deliver the entire social, political, and cultural context into the decision-making process. A profound level of cultural understanding is needed to turn survey results into effective communications programs. For example, in postmodern cultures, a message is better accepted when it promises to make the opinion adoptee look like an insightful individual who goes against the orthodoxy of the system. In traditional and modern societies, that kind of promise would have little appeal and might even be a liability. Because most developed countries contain both modern and postmodern segments,[22] a basic consideration in crafting a message–medium combination is the influence that various segments have with those who control resource access (e.g., government or a stakeholder network).

Where issues are involved, one of the most effective media is news coverage. The trick is to control its content. Here, too, creativity is required. Press releases alone have a very low probability of being publicized. However, creative publicity stunts can work wonders. For example, Greenpeace grew from living-room meetings to be a global corporation in less than a decade,[23] mostly because of its superb mastery of the publicity stunt. However, its base has not expanded beyond the postmodern segments of the developed world and the elites of the developing world, probably because the environment connects with very different values in traditional, modern, and postmodern societies, and the Greenpeace message is purely postmodern.[24]

Stakeholder Approach With Opinion Leaders

The distinction between the public opinion approach and the stakeholder and opinion leader approach can be compared to the two different paths to opinion formation discovered by social psychologists Richard Petty and John Cacioppo.[25] They showed that most opinions are absorbed unthinkingly, without the involvement of any analytic cognition. This is called the peripheral route to opinion formation. Because of the simple lack of time, we humans seldom go through the effort of collecting information, analyzing its validity, and thinking through the implications. However, when we do, it is a process Petty and Cacioppo called the central route to opinion formation.

Those who take the central route on an issue come to be known as opinion leaders. Others look to them for opinions in order to avoid doing all the difficult research and analysis themselves. Leaders of organizations must assume the role of opinion leaders when they speak on behalf of the organization. Part of their leadership role is to interpret events and information for the membership. They take the cognitive route so that the membership (e.g., employees or volunteers) can take the peripheral route. In order to maintain the legitimacy of their leadership, however, leaders usually must also accept bottom-up guidance. Part of their role is to articulate the opinions of the members. Because groups, rather than individuals, are the main actors in issue campaigns, it is very important to know what group leaders are thinking in order to influence the evolution of an issue.

The stakeholder network approach to issues management focuses on the ideas and sociopolitical networks of opinion leaders. They are the leverage points for change. As issues evolve, different organizations become active or inactive. Each organization leader brings a different set of ideas and resources to the network of those who actively affect the issue or who are actively affected by it. This approach ultimately requires the formation of alliances based on trust and cooperation. In the process, most of the goals of CSR, corporate sustainability, and corporate citizenship get fulfilled. There will always be critics, but the goal is to reduce their numbers to only those who have a reputation for rejecting collaboration toward the common good.

Legitimization in Stakeholder Networks

Today the overarching goal of issues management for organizations is to maintain a stable sociopolitical environment in which the governing entity, whoever or whatever that might be, grants legitimacy to organizations' resource access. This was not a big concern in the past because issues management was mostly practiced on the domestic scene in liberal democracies. In that context, there was already an informal social contract that legitimized each organization's role in society. However, with the declining effectiveness of the nation-state and the expansion of the economy to places that never had a durable social contract, priorities have changed. Organizations, especially corporations, are being challenged to relegitimize their roles. This is not done through any formal process. Rather, it is done issue by issue. Issues managers, therefore, have a central role to play in this process that can be characterized as the negotiation of a new social contract.

When an organization takes a proactive approach to the legitimacy of its resource access, crises are less likely, and when they do occur, they are less severe. A proactive, strategic approach means developing stakeholder relationships that have enough trust and understanding to forge a social contract on an issue. This is seldom achieved through pure philanthropy. It takes transactions that build trust around the matters related to the core of the organization's mission and reason for existence. The search for such relationships often provokes an internal debate with the organization regarding its citizenship role. When an organization knows what part it contributes to a functioning, just society, it knows how to win legitimacy for itself, even where the rule of law is thin.

Throughout the issue life cycle, building relationships with opinion leaders who have a stake in the issue contributes to building a network around the issue. When issues create crises for organizations, it is often because separate networks have formed. Each network has its own framing of the issue, its own justifications for members' actions, and its normative code for membership in the sociopolitical alliance. The stakeholder network approach aims to prevent the formation of detached networks in the first place. Where they have already occurred, it aims to meld the networks. This entails creating a unified frame for the issue and a unified code of member behavior. Such a code creates the groundwork for network governance and therefore makes it possible to relegitimize an organization's resource access.

In the following chapters, we will look at how to diagnose networks of stakeholders and issues. Issues and values can be viewed as linked to each other in networks, too. When we put these powerful techniques together, strategies immediately emerge for issue resolution.

Questions for Managers

A recurring theme in this chapter was the legitimization of your organization's access to resources. Think of an issue your organization has now, has had in the past, or could have in the future. Then ponder these questions:

- How could the issue prevent your organization from accessing vital resources? Which resources? Are they tangible or intangible? Would it be a complete loss of access or just more expensive access?
- What do the issue proponents consider illegitimate (in the broadest sense) about your organization's activities?
- Which best describes where the issue is now? Is it (a) being articulated, (b) being popularized, or (c) under study by a governance body?
- Is there a clear-cut, single institution with sovereign responsibility for regulating the issue? Does the issue involve several regulators and rule-setting organizations? Do aspects of it fall between the cracks? Is it something that none of the relevant authorities or institutions has ever had to deal with before?
- Do you know where the general public stands on the issue? If the public is divided into opinion segments, do you know who the opinion leaders are in each segment?

CHAPTER 3

Social Capital in Stakeholder Networks

In the previous chapter we talked rather loosely about networks of relationships. In this chapter we look at the concepts and distinctions needed to actually measure relationship strength and the level of sociopolitical risk in the environment. These kinds of measures are what make it possible to realistically assess the dynamics of an issue and develop strategies for managing it.

The goal of measuring relationship strength is ambitious. Relationships are multifaceted. There are hundreds of dimensions and qualities that one could potentially measure. How can we ever know which ones will matter for issues management?

What Is Social Capital and Why Does It Matter?

Collaborative Capacity in Relationships

In order to threaten the legitimacy of an organization's resource access, an issue has to enter the stage of political mobilization. Because political mobilization takes collaboration, there must be relationships that support collaboration. If we can measure the collaborative capacity in relationships, we can predict the sources of threats to resource access. Therefore, we need to measure whatever creates collaborative capacity in relationships. That "whatever" happens to be social capital.

Measuring the collaborative capacity of relationships (i.e., their social capital levels) would be enough in itself to suggest issue management strategies. However, it would be a bonus if we could also measure (a) the levels of support each network actor accords to a company and its resource access and (b) the strength of association between various conceptual elements of the issue's framing. Fortunately, these measures are rather straightforward. The measurement of collaborative capacity in relationships presents the greatest challenge. For that reason, this chapter focuses on understanding the concept of social capital.

Measuring social capital is central to issue management because when you know the social capital patterns in the stakeholder network, you can change the shape of the network to one that gives you a more stable, lower risk sociopolitical environment.

Debate Over Definitions

The first step in measurement is always to make sure you know what you are trying to measure. This requires having a clear definition of the concept. Attempts to define social capital have produced a literature that includes participants from diverse disciplines. The majority of the participants are sociologists, development economists, and political scientists, but there are also participants who contribute to fields such as history, philosophy, public health, and management science.[1]

To summarize the history of the usage and meaning of the term, before the 1970s, "social capital" was used as an evocative term to blend a sense of hard economics with soft social resources. In the 1970s and 1980s, sociologists and economists began making formal distinctions among economic capital, or financial capital as it is also called; human capital; social capital; and cultural capital. In the 1990s, political scientists loosened the meaning of the term when they began talking about social capital as a characteristic of societies and nations. Meanwhile, social network analysts in sociology strove to give the term more precision. The ensuing confusion produced several critiques. There was generally more dissatisfaction with the political science definitions than with the network definitions.

At the same time, management theorists began advocating for more definitional precision in their attempts to apply social capital to the understanding of organizations. Two definitions deserve special attention because together they highlight what we need to know in applying the concept to issues management. In the first, British management theorists Janine Nahapiet and the late Sumantra Ghoshal postulated three dimensions to social capital. The structural dimension subsumed the entire network view of social capital. The two content dimensions were the relational and cognitive. The relational was mostly a matter of trust and its associated qualities, such as reciprocity and mutual identification. According to Nahapiet and Ghoshal, the cognitive dimension depends on shared language, frameworks, goals, and visions for the future.[2]

The second noteworthy definition of social capital came from U.S.-based management theorists Paul Adler and Seok-Woo Kwon. They went further in separating the sources and consequences of social capital from its core in order to avoid circular arguments. They defined it as "the goodwill available to individuals or groups. Its source lies in the structure and content of the actor's social relations. Its effects flow from the information, influence, and solidarity it makes available to the actor."[3]

For Adler and Kwon, the three dimensions identified by Nahapiet and Ghoshal would qualify as sources of social capital. The core is goodwill, which gives the actor information, influence, and solidarity, which in turn produce further effects. Note that what must be measured in this definition is goodwill in social relations, which could be construed as a product of the three dimensions identified by Nahapiet and Ghoshal. Note also that Adler and Kwon see information, influence, and solidarity as effects, albeit effects so immediate that they are used to characterize the aspect of goodwill that matters. The point of splitting these hairs is to avoid circular reasoning. The aspect of the definitions we choose to measure must not be later taken to be effects of social capital. For example, if we measure social capital as goodwill, we cannot later conclude that goodwill produces social capital. It *is* social capital by operational definition.

Figure 3.1 shows a way to integrate the definition of Nahapiet and Ghoshal with the definition of Adler and Kwon. The sources column on the left shows Nahapiet and Ghoshal's three dimensions in simple language. The relational dimension is labeled in Figure 3.1 as quality of relationships. It involves large components of trust and mutuality, which are central to attributions of a high-quality relationship. The cognitive dimension is labeled as shared understanding. It involves shared mental models, ranging from language and culture to technical paradigm. For that reason, it is described as shared understanding. The structural dimension is labeled as structure of network. It refers to social capital gained through various types of centrality in a network. These three qualities produce goodwill in relationships between pairs of network participants. The goodwill is manifested as Adler and Kwon's three

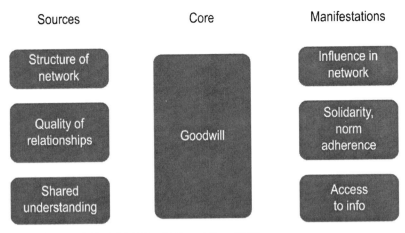

Note: Nahapiet and Ghoshal (1998) and Adler and Kwon (2002).

Figure 3.1. Integration of definitions of social capital.

benefits of social capital, namely, information access, solidarity, and influence.

Social capital is often distinguished from human capital (i.e., abilities, health, and knowledge) and cultural capital (i.e., rituals, practices, cultural knowledge, and artifacts). In recent years, several other kinds of nonfinancial capital have also been proposed.[4] Social capital, however, has received far more attention than the others. Perhaps what makes social capital so difficult to define is its manifestation in such a vast range of fields. In addition to its ubiquitous use in most of the social sciences, it seems to have correlates in human physiology and the study of primate behavior.[5] It seems that social capital is an aspect of human behavior rooted in the primordial past. In any case, conceptualizing and defining it seems to require integrating findings ranging from brain physiology to history. The effort to define it will likely continue for some time.

What Social Capital Buys at Each Stage of the Issue Life Cycle

Social capital is essential at every stage of the issue life cycle. In the first stage, when the issue is being articulated and framed, social capital brings together the right combination of human and cultural capital needed to craft an issue frame that could have broad appeal.

In the social movement or campaigning stage, social capital can be used to directly influence the opinions of others. However, its more strategic use is to influence the opinions of opinion leaders. This is the use of social capital to create sociopolitical alliances. The collaboration needed to develop an alliance depends on high levels of social capital among the leaders of the groups involved. As networks of networks adopt the frame, it eventually reaches a threshold where it becomes public knowledge.

When an issue reaches the stage where whatever governs must take account of it, social capital is needed to coordinate a response. Where governments govern, the policy developers need to understand the social capital among all the internal and external stakeholders in order to craft a policy that will be accepted. The last thing they want is to hand a potent alliance over to their political opponents. Where the rule of law is thin and governance defaults to whatever can be agreed upon by a network of stakeholders, the campaigning continues indefinitely until the alliances stabilize around a consensus that can be turned into a network norm. This is not an automatic or guaranteed outcome. Only particular kinds of network structures will permit this to happen. Shaping the stakeholder network into one of these structures requires knowledge of the social capital among all the stakeholders.

Through the whole process, social capital is used by all the different stakeholders to get information, influence, and the conformity of others to the group's norms. Understanding the channels through which information, influence, and solidarity flow gives one a vantage point from which superior strategies can be developed. Risks and opportunities are written in the patterns of social capital in stakeholder networks.

Patterns of Social Capital

Early Typologies of Social Capital's Patterns in Networks

Research on the sociopolitical implications of social capital took two distinct paths at the turn of the 21st century. Those interested in its effects on democracy and prosperity tended to use random sample surveys and government statistics to gauge the prevalence of membership in civic organizations.[6] The hypothesis was that such organizations created ties across groups that would otherwise remain unconnected (e.g., racial groups, ethnic groups, and social classes).

Those interested in social capital as a factor in poverty reduction tended to study village- or regional-level cases and paid closer attention to the patterns of ties among the actors and organizations. The concepts of "bridging social capital" and "bonding social capital" were developed to describe two different patterns that complemented each other and promoted community development.[7] Bonding refers to a pattern in which everyone knows everyone and has strong ties (e.g., frequent contact, high levels of trust, and shared cognitive frameworks). Bridging refers to ties that link otherwise unconnected, bonded subgroups. The World Bank funded several studies in developing countries using this network-oriented, case study approach. This branch of social capital research not only confirmed the importance of bonding and bridging but also highlighted a third pattern: linking social capital. According to the typology of social capital patterns proposed by Michael Woolcock and colleagues, linking is a type of bridging that connects a group to those with resources and power outside the region or at a higher level of organization.[8]

Figure 3.2 shows examples of bonding, bridging, and linking configurations in a network graph. The circles represent stakeholder groups. The lines represent relationships high in social capital. There are two bonded groups: A-B-C-D-E and G-H-I-J-K. The individual members of these groups, and the groups themselves as units, both have a high level of bonding social capital. The tie between actor A and actor K is a bridging relationship. Actors A and K enjoy high bridging social capital because they have better access to the information and resources of the other group. This gives them unique resources within their own group. Actor F is a bridging actor. He has access to the resources of both bonded groups but does not enjoy any bonding social capital of his own. He has high bridging social capital and low bonding social capital.

In the bonding-bridging-linking typology of social capital patterns, actors A to K all operate in the same local region. They are like two villages. Actors L-M-N operate at higher levels of jurisdiction or geography. They have access to resources from a broader network. They could be departments of a national government, international nongovernmental organizations, or internationally active corporations. The advantage of linking social capital for poverty reduction is that it breaks the isolation

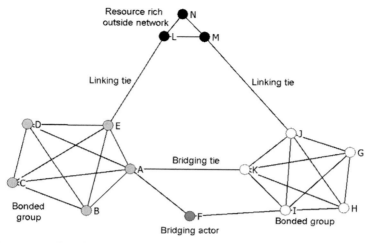

Figure 3.2. Bonding, bridging, and linking social capital.

of the villages and gives them access to broader markets, outside aid and finance, and better technology and human capital development opportunities.

This line of network-oriented social capital research led to thinking about what kinds of network patterns and governance structures lead to effective collaboration among the poor. The bonding was deemed important for collective action. The bridging was deemed important to avoid intergroup conflict. The linking was seen as important for the financial efficiencies and opportunities it brings.

Subsequent research has illustrated how linking allows a community to enter an international supply chain, thereby enormously expanding the market for its resources and capabilities while simultaneously giving it access to productivity-enhancing tools and ideas. Several economists see this dynamic as an explanation for why poor communities in developing countries have generally benefited from globalization to a historically unprecedented extent both in terms of reduced absolute and relative poverty.[9] In development economics, corporations came to be seen as important participants in the processes that reduce global poverty and global inequality.

Why should organizational issues managers care about network structures that reduce poverty? All the various reasons will become clear throughout this book. For now, it is sufficient to note two. First, corporate-based issues managers should care because the reduction of poverty and the promotion of prosperity are at the core of legitimizing the role of business in society. Bridging, bonding, and linking social capital give corporations resource access while creating prosperity for stakeholders who control access to the resources. Issues managers will occasionally find their company's access to resources challenged by anticorporate critics who portray their resource assess as exploitive. However, research has shown that expanding resource access by corporations, along with increased bridging, bonding, and linking, social capital are central in the process by which global resource access has contributed to the conversion of hundreds of millions of the world's historic poor into the new global middle class. Because of economic globalization, the 20th-century alarm over mass famine has been replaced by the 21st-century alarm over mass automobile ownership. Second, bonding, bridging, and linking are invaluable tools in managing stakeholder issues. They help create mature sociopolitical environments where facts count, due process is followed, and rights are respected. All these things make the sociopolitical environment less risky. They are environments in which issues managers and stakeholders can more readily formulate shared goals and collaborate toward achieving them.

More recently, researchers in management and organizational science have looked at the importance of bridging and bonding patterns of social capital in diverse areas such as organizational development, entrepreneurship, innovation, theories of the firm, and interfirm alliances.[10] I myself took the network approach a step further in devising a typology of stakeholder network patterns.[11] The revised typology presented in the next section associates various patterns of social capital in stakeholder networks with common obstacles and opportunities in stakeholder issues management.

A More Advanced Typology of Social Capital Patterns in Networks

Social capital in networks can create accountability and norm adherence,[12] which are essential elements of governance and the legitimization of an organization's activities. Networks have the capacity to resolve issues and controversies by creating accords that function where the rule of law is thin or where jurisdiction is disputed.[13]

Despite the advantages of network governance, there are also pitfalls. Network governance can fail through the development of an us-versus-them dynamic. Therefore, it is wise to use market and hierarchical governance at the same time. This can be a challenge. For one thing, different cultures have different preferences for the domination of one governance mechanism over another.[14] Another challenge is to avoid situations in which different governance mechanisms push behavior in contradictory directions, unless this is deliberately done to have one governance force provide a counterbalance or limitation on the direction encouraged by the other.

Although the concepts of bridging and bonding are useful in understanding how to foster network governance, they are limited. More comprehensive tools are needed to take advantage of the opportunities and to avoid the pitfalls. To that end, the typology of network patterns shown in Figure 3.3 contains nine distinct network patterns, or templates. The typology has vertical and horizontal dimensions. They are refinements of the concepts of bridging and bonding. The basic idea is that one can have social capital by being an equal among equals or, conversely, that one can have social capital by having a superior portfolio of connections.

The vertical dimension in Figure 3.3 corresponds to the degree of bonding in the network, but the more technical term is the degree of closure of the network. It represents the social capital of belonging and cohesiveness.

The horizontal dimension takes the bridging concept to the extreme in an attempt to articulate a source of social capital completely opposite to bonding. The horizontal axis indexes the core–periphery structure of a network. It is the extent to which one person has monopolized all the flows of influence and information. A person, or a small group of people, can be the sole bridge in the network only if none of the other actors in the network has ties with others. In this case, the bridger is called a core and everyone else is classified as the periphery. The absence of bonding among periphery members makes the bridging pattern antithetical to bonding. In the extreme, the core acts as the gatekeeper for everything that flows through the network (e.g., information and resources). Bridging yields brokerage opportunities and higher information access. This level of power can raise the core's social and political status, but because it comes with a lack of accountability, it can also foster corruption.[15]

The core–periphery concept subsumes bridging. What is bridged in bridging is a space between two actors, or groups of actors, where no ties exist. The technical term for this space is a "structural hole."[16] The more structural holes one has in one's personal network, the less one is bound by the norms of any one group, and the more freedom one has to pick and choose relationships through which to seek resources. Moreover, one is also in a position to broker resources between groups or among actors.[17] These advantages are distinct aspects of social capital in networks. They are still goodwill that yields information, influence, and (some) solidarity, in accordance with Adler and Kwon's definition. They are still based on structural position (i.e., bridge), trust (by the bridged), and shared understanding (that the bridger has with all the various actors bridged to). Therefore, they are social capital. Nonetheless they tend to benefit the ones doing the bridging rather than directly benefiting all the members of the group, as is more the case with the social capital produced by bonding.

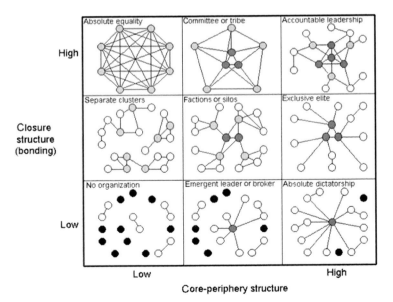

Figure 3.3. Typology of network configurations by level of bonding and core–periphery structure.

The bridging in a core–periphery structure is not limited to an individual. An entire bonded group of social actors can bridge among other social actors outside the group. The core–periphery concept also permits the notion of a semiperiphery that does bridging on behalf of the bonded core group. The semiperiphery can create a smoother gradient of influence and inclusiveness from the core to the periphery. By contrast, a core with rigid in-group boundaries can operate as an exclusive self-serving elite. Although this begins to overlap with the notion of hierarchy, the core–periphery concept by definition does not presuppose any formal organization or authority structure whatsoever.[18]

The typology in Figure 3.3 identifies which network configurations risk excessive bonding and excessively sharp divisions between the core and the periphery. By comparing existing or proposed governance networks with those configurations, it is possible to devise strategies to improve them. The vertical dimension of the typology ranges from low to high bonding. The horizontal dimension ranges from no core–periphery structure on the left to a sharply defined core–periphery structure on the right.

The nine cells of Figure 3.3 show nine templates, or stylized network structures, that illustrate combinations of bonding and core–periphery structures. The black circles represent groups with no connections to others. In technical language, they are "social isolates." The dark gray circles represent the cores of their networks. The white circles represent members of the periphery. The light gray circles represent either semiperiphery actors or those who are simultaneously core and periphery. The lines between the actors represent their relationships.

Implications of Templates for Governance and Issues Management

The cells at the extremes of the two dimensions in Figure 3.3 will be contrasted first (i.e., top left and bottom right). Then we will consider the case where they are both absent (i.e., no organization), in order to show the progression along the vertical and horizontal axes. Then we look at the case where they are both high (i.e., accountable leadership). That will be followed by a look at the cells along the high rows and columns for each dimension (i.e., absolute equality to accountable leadership and absolute dictatorship to accountable leadership). Finally, the center cell will be discussed in relation to the diagonal progression from no organization to accountable leadership.

Absolute Equality

The top-left template in Figure 3.3, labeled "absolute equality," is the extreme of bonding without any core or periphery. All of the members of the network have social ties with each other. Because the pattern has neither a core nor a periphery, all the actors are colored light gray. Structurally speaking, they are equals. They can easily monitor each other's behavior and punish norm violators. The internal homogeneity, however, can lead to everyone having the same ideas. Moreover, if everyone gets a veto, the probability of network-wide innovation is further depressed. After analyzing community networks, Jenny Onyx and Paul Bullen warn that although bonding can create social order, excessive bonding can create parochial prejudice against outsiders and minorities.[19]

In issues management, a stakeholder network with this structure would indicate the absence of controversy in the sense that everyone has the same opinion. However, if this were a subcluster of stakeholders in a larger network, it would indicate a group absolutely convinced of the correctness of its opinions. If they were supportive of the focal organization's access to resources, they might have trouble being open enough to accept creative governance and legitimization solutions that would include other stakeholders questioning the focal organization's resource access. They would not see any need for a relegitimization of the access. Similarly, if this were a subcluster of stakeholders opposed to the focal organization's resource access, they would not understand any perspectives divergent from their own. Anything short of withdrawing the organization's social license to operate (SLO) would seem unthinkable.

The most obvious strategy in such cases would be to foster more high-social capital relationships (i.e., based on trust and shared understanding) between members of this subcluster and stakeholders with different ideas. In other words, at least some of the members of an absolute equality subcluster would be encouraged to participate in bridging relationships outside their group.

Absolute Dictatorship

The bottom-right template (absolute dictatorship) is the extreme of a core–periphery structure with a single actor monopolizing all the flows in the network. The core is completely free from accountability because the periphery members cannot compare observations among themselves. They have been divided and conquered. However, this pattern is also optimal for quick, albeit arbitrary, decision making and action and for access to unfiltered information from numerous sources. It permits more rapid assimilation of novelty and diversity, albeit at the cost of subordination of the periphery to the norms imposed by the core.

In issues management, the core is likely to decide whether an issue exists or not. If the core approves of the focal organization's activities, there will be no controversy. If the core disapproves, the issue goes straight to the stage of governance intervention, which in this case means that the core makes whatever changes it likes to the organization's resource access. For example, the core might decide to confiscate the resource, as the government of Venezuela did with the Las Cristinas gold mine.[20] Indeed, political scientists debate a version of the "natural resource curse" hypothesis, which says that valuable natural resources, such as oil, that shift government revenues away from a dependence on taxes paid by citizens, cause a drift toward authoritarian government.[21] Authoritarian government creates a network structure similar to the absolute dictator template in Figure 3.3.

The absolute dictatorship can also present sociopolitical risk when it supports the focal organization's activities but the periphery does not. In this case, the focal organization is perceived to be an ally of the dictator. Should members of the periphery somehow close the structural holes that separate them, their united front could create an issue for the focal organization very rapidly and violently. The dictator's friends tend to get overthrown along with the dictator.

The general issue management strategy in this case is to align the views of the core and periphery. Even though popular legitimization for the focal organization's activities might not be important to the core, it might not be objectionable either. In that case, initiatives to show the members of the periphery what is in it for them would reduce the risk of a crisis issue in the future. In some circumstances, the focal organization might be able to smooth the gradient between the core and the periphery—that is, a semiperiphery (e.g., the middle class) could be encouraged, which ideally would help spread the benefits enjoyed by the core to wider segments of the stakeholder network. This, too, would reduce the risk of an explosive issue crisis in the longer term.

No Organization

The bottom-left template in Figure 3.3 (no organization) shows the absence of both bonding and core–periphery structure. This template would be typical of a community after a civil war, natural disaster, or dictatorship. It has very little social capital.

With no social capital, there is very little chance that an issue could move to the second stage of political action to mobilize a campaign against the focal organization. However, that does not mean the sociopolitical risk is necessarily low. It is only low if the focal organization's activities do not create a reason for the stakeholders to connect with one another. However, if the focal organization brings the promise of wealth (e.g., job, royalties) or the threat of damage (e.g., environmental or health), then this network pattern will change very quickly.

Nature abhors a power vacuum. That is why the "no organization" structure can be the least stable, least predictable pattern. It can quickly evolve into any of its adjacent cells. Therefore, the most prudent issues management strategy is to take an active role in facilitating the creation of community among the stakeholders. Indeed, this can be the ideal situation for building long-lasting, mutually rewarding relationships. However, there is no way to avoid politics at the community level. Research on the politics of primate species suggests that part of our inheritance from our prehuman forbearers is an innate tendency to engage in politics.[22] Although creating a community automatically creates the conditions for conflicting interests, the conflicts do not automatically need to revolve around the legitimacy of the focal organization's activities. A large part of establishing and maintaining such legitimacy from the start depends on enshrining collaborative norms (e.g., mutual benefit, reciprocity, and respect) in the foundations of the relationships.

Separate Clusters

The "separate clusters" template appears halfway between the "no organization" pattern and the "perfect equality" pattern. The template depicts a stakeholder network with social capital but with no core. These types of ties among stakeholders are likely to be based on proximity or frequency of contact more than anything else. The structure suggests a high level of self-sufficiency that removes any need for developing a higher order structure for sharing resources and energy. All stakeholders have calculated that there is no reward big enough to justify expending the resources and effort that would be required to maneuver oneself into a core position.

Issues management in this situation is likely to require a different approach for each cluster. This could mean more work. It also multiplies the number of separate contexts in which issues could arise. Unless there is some extraneous reason for these separate clusters to exist, the most obvious strategy would be to unite them into a single network with an accountable core. This would give the stakeholders the ability to speak with one voice based on matters of genuine shared interest. For the focal organization, it would reduce the cost of effective communications and would probably stabilize the sociopolitical environment by bringing all clusters under one set of norms and one shared leadership structure.

Emergent Leader or Broker

The bottom-center template (emergent leader or broker) sits at an intermediate point between no organization and absolute dictatorship. It is a pattern with an emerging core but very little bonding. The principle point of contention in this type pattern is likely to be the core's legitimacy as a representative for all the stakeholders. From the descriptions we have of the Shell controversy with the Ogoni in Nigeria,[23] the Ogoni people were not organized collectively when Shell first arrived. The situation most closely matched the "no organization" pattern. Eventually, an activist named Ken Saro-Wiwa set up an umbrella organization called the Movement for the Survival of the Ogoni People (MOSOP). His aim was for MOSOP to represent all the Ogoni. Therefore, the stakeholder network appeared to have evolved into an "emergent leader or broker" pattern.

Shell spent years denying the legitimacy of Saro-Wiwa's attempts to speak for the Ogoni. In 1995, the military regime of Nigeria executed Saro-Wiwa. International activists accused Shell of complicity. Shell denied any responsibility and in 2009 paid the Ogoni US$15.5 million to settle a case based on those accusations.[24]

What would have been a better strategy? The stakeholder network was heading toward an absolute dictatorship pattern. However, a split in MOSOP proved that alternate points of view were starting to get organized. To prevent a drift toward absolute dictatorship, Shell could have encouraged more social capital among the stakeholders so that no one person could claim to speak for everyone unless they had truly earned the consensual support of everyone. Instead, Shell used the emergence of alternative voices as an excuse to do nothing. It was as if Shell did not see itself as a stakeholder in the shared problem of Ogoni sociopolitical development. It apparently did not see its corporate citizenship as including the responsibility to participate in community social-capital building.

Accountable Leadership

The top-right template in Figure 3.3 (accountable leadership) has a galaxy shape. It also has a smooth gradient from the core to the periphery in terms of the number of connections maintained by the actors in each successive ring. The core is bonded, but the bonding is not exclusive. It includes the semiperiphery. Each semiperiphery member enjoys some bridging benefits with respect to the peripheral members of its wing. Moreover, the periphery and semiperiphery are connected enough that they can enforce accountability upon the core.

This template shows a desirable balance of bonding and core–periphery structure. The network is inclusive yet has a core strong enough to impose norms and accountability. As partial bridgers, the semiperiphery members have more freedom of action, social mobility, and potential for innovation.

Issue management in a stakeholder network like this is much easier than with the other patterns because the network is already capable of adapting its internal social contract in order to assimilate new information and practices while legitimately articulating both its fundamental values and its short-term negotiating positions. It presents a stable sociopolitical environment where the rule of law is probably respected. There are always critics, and political gamesmanship will never end, but in this environment there are also well-enforced rules for conflict resolution. For example, libel, slander, threats, assaults, and kidnappings are so unacceptable that they delegitimize those who use them and actually decrease the user's chances of success.

In this type of environment, the challenges are mostly in communications planning and relationship building. Fortunately, there are already well-tested systems for rising to the challenges. This predictability gives issue managers the free capacity to focus on finer points of stakeholder network management. For example, there is time to go into more depth on how issues are related to one another and what possible overlaps exist at the level of shared values among stakeholders and their issues. In addition, it is possible to design initiatives that would raise the focal organization's level of SLO to the level of approval or identification.

Committee or Tribe

The "committee or tribe" pattern (top center) is halfway between absolute equality and accountable leadership. Although all the members of the network know each other, the pattern includes a rudimentary leadership. This core is not much more powerful than its surrounding periphery but may at least be able to set an agenda. They also make obvious choices for participants in the bridges they maintain with outside groups.

One advantage of this pattern is that the leadership has impeccable legitimacy and accountability. All the members know what the leaders know. Transparency is near perfect. Another advantage is the capacity of the group to collaborate. With such high bonding, the group is capable of launching coordinated action immediately.

A disadvantage of this pattern of stakeholder network is its isolation. It suffers from the same conformity as the "absolute equality" pattern and the same suspiciousness toward outsiders and new ideas. The very cohesiveness of the group retards its innovative capacity. It often takes a crisis to get change accepted in a stakeholder network like this. At the same time, when the group consensus starts down a high-risk line of thought, the effects of groupthink make members oblivious to the risks.[25]

Issues management in a stakeholder network with a committee or tribe pattern requires creating opportunities for in-depth discussions of the issues. These might require delving into the unarticulated assumptions behind the beliefs, positions, anxieties, and aspirations surrounding the issue. Quite often issues managers begin by giving this type of network a barrage of facts without realizing that there is not agreement on what constitutes a valid argument or a valid decision process. To some extent, the issue manager must become an anthropologist in order to understand how to communicate with stakeholders in this type of configuration. Once effective communication is established, progress toward collaboration can move quite smoothly. As mentioned, the stakeholders are ready and able to act in concert once they agree on goals.

Exclusive Elite

The "exclusive elite" pattern is halfway between the absolute dictatorship pattern and the accountable leadership pattern. The core consists of a bonded group. It is dictatorship by an elite. The pattern shares the advantages of dictatorship in terms of being able to make bold changes quickly and to govern and take advantage of resources from diverse corners of the network. Moreover, because it is a whole class of stakeholders, it has the capacity to reproduce itself and maintain the position of privilege over generations.

The disadvantages are many. The elite core, like the absolute dictator, is haunted by temptations to disregard human rights for its own benefit. The abrupt gap in resources between the elite and the periphery can easily lead to a huge waste of human resources in the periphery. Moreover, it can create conditions that foment the sudden overthrow of the elite.

In terms of issue management, the risks are similar to those of an absolute dictatorship. However, they can be more subtle. A very common strategic mistake made by Western companies entering a foreign country with a stark class system is to seek social and cultural capital to get things done. To that end, the company hires a member of the local elite to be their political fixer. Typically, the person has a Western education, speaks

English well (i.e., has cultural capital to bridge cultures), and comes from a politically well-connected national family (i.e., has social capital).

The strategy amounts to subcontracting out the company's issues management. However, it runs the risk of embedding the company in the subculture of the local elite. The elite may not operate in accordance with the highest principles of social responsibility as enunciated in the company's sustainability report. It is worthwhile to study the history of the country to find out how they became the elite. Too often, the company finds it has become an instrument for perpetuating the injustices of the past. Moreover, the company risks being exploited by the elite. By delegating the management of its social and cultural capital to a small clique of bridging actors, the company operates in ignorance. The bridging actors often filter information. Such companies miss opportunities to learn about things such as lower cost local suppliers (i.e., human capital) and lower cost procedures that circumvent the involvement of the elite (i.e., cultural capital). Relationships cannot be outsourced.

These risks are not diminished by putting members of the local elite on the payroll. As employees, elites are even more likely to damage the company's reputation with local stakeholders because (a) they feel they will have the backing of the company in any disputes and (b) they tell local stakeholders that they are acting on behalf of the company even when what they do is contrary to company corporate social responsibility (CSR) and sustainability guidelines. The establishment of high–social capital relationships with stakeholders must be done by members of the focal organization who put CSR and sustainability policy into practice. Anyone can reassure the boss that everything is being done according to the CSR and sustainability policy. Unfortunately, experience shows that when the person doing the reassuring is a member of a local elite, the boss should more often verify the reassurances.[26]

Factions or Silos

In the template in the middle of Figure 3.3 (factions or silos), the core is surrounded by factions that are each nearly as powerful as each core member. This makes it difficult for the core to enforce norms. This pattern would likely be associated with power struggles among rival factions. The four periphery groups are like silos. Without a core strong enough to enforce norms, the pattern could easily deteriorate into mutual attacks among the factions. Moreover, because each faction is internally bonded, it seeks only the benefit of its own members. This can produce rent-seeking alliances.

The factions or silos pattern lies on the diagonal between no organization and accountable leadership. The diagonal loosely parallels the history of Europe from the Treaty of Westphalia to the European Union. First there were separate states. Before the ink was dry, there were alliances fighting for more control (the factions or silos pattern). This went on for over three centuries. Then a core developed that was strong enough to impose regional norms and standards.

In terms of core–periphery structure, the silo pattern is also halfway between separate clusters and exclusive elite. There is an intermediate level of bonding in all these patterns (i.e., the exclusive elite features bonding in the core), but they vary in terms of the strength of the core. The separate clusters pattern has no core. The factions or silos pattern has a weak core. The exclusive elite has a strong core. At the end of the period of Chinese history known as the Zhou dynasty, China had a factions or silos structure. The core was weak and seven states ruled by warlords were on the rise. This is when Confucius lived.[27] As the silo structure deteriorated into the Warring States period (475–221 BC) with no core at all, Confucius's philosophy of order and harmony grew in popularity.

The factions or silos pattern is also halfway between the emergent leader or broker pattern and the committee or tribe. All three have cores that are weak or not firmly established. In the emergent leader or broker pattern, the periphery is unconnected (low in bonding). In the factions or silos pattern, the periphery has bonding at a local level but the whole network continues to show structural holes between the bonded clusters. In the committee or tribe pattern, the structural holes in the periphery have disappeared. This vertical progression is loosely analogous to the middle stages of work-group development. Groups are said to go through the four stages of forming (coming together to form the group), storming (power struggles over direction and leadership), norming (agreeing of procedural norms), and performing.[28] In Figure 3.3, the movement from no organization to emergent leadership is analogous to forming. The movement from emergent leadership to factions or silos is analogous to storming. The movement from factions or silos to committee or tribe is analogous to norming. Finally, the movement from committee or tribe to accountable leadership is analogous to performing.

In terms of issues management, the factions or silos pattern is the most difficult. The core is not strong enough to impose norms. If this pattern emerges in an area where the rule of law is thin, stakeholders may resort to tactics such as murder, kidnapping, threats, extortion, libel, blockades, occupations, and the deliberate dissemination of false information. The line between social mobilization and feuding becomes fuzzy.

Recovering from these, or preventing a slide into them, requires increasing the network's intergroup social capital one relationship at a time. The attenuation of the us-versus-them thinking that characterizes highly bonded groups can be aided by both the development of an integrative core and the creation of trusting bonds among the bonded groups. The emergence of common ground on issues parallels the emergence of intergroup trust.

Assessing the Issue Environment

Matching Templates to Real Stakeholder Networks

Each of these nine templates has a different potential for balancing freedom and social control, enforceable norms and tolerance for diversity, and accountability and innovation. Actual stakeholder networks can be compared with these stylized templates. Where similarities are found, interventions can be designed to reshape the existing network in a more desired direction.

The actual networks might be specific industries and their stakeholders (e.g., investment banks and credit-rating agencies) or networks of organizations with stakes in shared global problem domains (e.g., international health agencies). Different levels of sociogeographic inclusiveness may need different structures because some of the patterns in Figure 3.3 (e.g., absolute equality and committee or tribe) are impossible in very large groups.[29] In addition, the interactions among layers of networks need attention. For example, it may be possible to compensate for lower accountability in one layer by choosing higher accountability patterns for the layers above and below it.

At the global level of governance, the combination of markets and formal hierarchies is not sufficient. Further work on classifying network governance alternatives might provide practical guidance for avoiding excesses. For example, when stakeholders dispute which kinds of institutional arrangements should be put in place to create accountability, the typology might be used as a criterion to rule out certain suggestions.

Measuring Social Capital

The strategic power of the typology in Figure 3.3 highlights the advantages of measuring the patterns of social capital among stakeholders in an issue network. The definitions of social capital offered by Nahapiet and Ghoshal and by Adler and Kwon (merged in Figure 3.1) provide a sound starting point for deciding exactly what to measure. There are two advantages of focusing on Adler and Kwon's goodwill rather than their information, influence, and solidarity.

First, the latter are outcomes that we would like to predict when we analyze stakeholder networks in the service of issue management. Measuring them directly would only predict their reoccurrence in a partial way and in a stable network. If we focus on their sources instead, which to Adler and Kwon is goodwill in networks, then we stand a better chance of being able to predict who will give information to whom, who will be able to influence whom, and who will abide by the norms espoused by whom.

Second, Adler and Kwon's goodwill overlaps considerably with Nahapiet and Ghoshal's three dimensions of social capital (i.e., structural, relational, and cognitive). Nahapiet and Ghoshal's structural dimension subsumes the vertical and horizontal dimensions in Figure 3.3. As argued previously, these have enormous predictive potential and therefore would be desirable inclusions in any measure aimed at developing issues management strategies.

Third, the relational dimension (i.e., reciprocity, trust, and identification) and the cognitive dimension (i.e., shared paradigms and goals) appear to capture the important dimensions of relationship quality more than things such as information exchange, influence, and solidarity. Indeed, even before the term "social capital" became popular in the social sciences, social network analysts were routinely measuring the friendship ties (relational) and advice-seeking (cognitive) ties in networks and finding different structures based on each.[30]

Therefore, in the next chapter we look in more detail at predictive-oriented methods for social capital stakeholder networks. Specifically, we focus on Nahapiet and Ghoshal's three dimensions.

Social capital in stakeholder networks tells us where the power, influence, and collaborative capacity are located. However, for issues management we need to supplement this with a broader view of the sociopolitical risk in the stakeholder environment. In the next chapter, we will also discuss how to use qualitative measures to gather this information. Then we will briefly look at a measure of the level of SLO. In chapter 6 we examine ways of combining all these perspectives in order to develop sociopolitical risk-management strategies.

Questions for Managers

This chapter explained the importance of knowing the level and distribution of social capital among the relationships in your stakeholder network. The following questions might spur some insights about how to apply these concepts right away to an issue of immediate concern:

- Which of the stakeholders advocating for issues affecting your organization have collaborative relationships with each other?
- Are there clusters of stakeholder on various sides of the issue? If so, which groups bridge between or among the clusters?
- Which of the nine templates describes the patterns and dynamics that have developed in interactions on the issue? Is there a small in-group calling the shots? Are there bonded clusters? If so, do they interact? Are they rivals?

CHAPTER 4

Getting the Data

Identifying and Prioritizing the Stakeholders for Interviewing

Obtaining data on the patterns of social capital in stakeholder issue networks requires interviewing the stakeholders. This chapter explains the details of an approach to interviewing that the author and colleagues have found effective. It includes standard social network techniques, standard qualitative techniques, and some innovations in the assessment of sociopolitical sentiments in a stakeholder context. The author conducts this type of research under the trademarked name of Stakeholder 360. It is only the name that is trademarked: Anyone can use the techniques described here. However, a license must be obtained from the author in order to call it Stakeholder 360.

The definition of "stakeholder" explains who should be interviewed. Stakeholders are those who are affected by the issue or who can have an effect upon the issue. Again, the issue may concern the activities of a particular focal organization or it may be a mess. A "mess" is a technical term in management theory that refers to a problem that can only be solved through the voluntary collaboration and cooperation of many organizations from many socioeconomic sectors.[1]

As argued in chapter 2, the opinions of the leaders of organizations represent the most strategic observation point for assessing the sociopolitical landscape. Occasionally there can be individual opinion leaders as well. For example, individual experts in universities, individual elected representatives (e.g., state assembly members and senators), or individual informal leaders (e.g., leaders of prominent local families or clans) can be opinion leaders when they speak out on issues. Therefore, the question of who to interview becomes a matter of making a list of the organizations and individuals who are affected or who can affect the issue.

Deciding Who to Interview

There are four main sources of names for the list of stakeholders to be interviewed:

1. Employees of the focal organization(s)
2. Media searches
3. Key informants used in social impact analysis
4. Recommendations from interviewed stakeholders (i.e., snowball sampling)

Employees of the Focal Organizations

When the issue revolves around the activities of a focal organization (e.g., employment practices or environmental performance), the employees responsible for dealing with the issue can usually name the most active and vocal stakeholders. These stakeholders identify themselves through their active promotion of the issue. When the issue is a mess, there are likely to be a handful of central organizations whose employees could collectively supply names. Typical organizations, for example, would include municipal governments, major employers or industry associations, state or provincial departments, journalists, and prominent community groups or educational institutions.

However, many issues are multifaceted and involve stakeholders who might not even know they are at risk of being affected. This is especially true when the issue is a mess, such as the issue of how to spark economic growth in a rural region. For example, owners of small farms around a village many not even realize that economic growth in the region would change the optimal use profile of their farmland. Therefore, additional techniques are needed to compile the stakeholder list.

Media Searches

If the issue has moved into the sphere of public discussion, there are likely media reports on it. These reports usually contain the names of knowledgeable individuals and concerned groups. The media to be scanned should include local newspapers, local broadcast outlets, and online media (e.g., organization websites, blogs, and news sites). Before starting any interviews, an Internet search should be conducted on the names of all the organizations and individuals already listed. This may turn up more names.

Be sure to bookmark sites that provide information and commentary on the issue. These will prove useful in the analysis of the qualitative data that will be collected.

Key Informants Used in Social Impact Assessment

Key informant interviews are often overlooked when trying to identify stakeholders. This is unfortunate because, as with other social impact analysis methods, it is very good for discovering less obvious stakeholders.

Social impact assessment[2] is a collection of techniques all aimed at discovering who is being, or would be, impacted by a proposed project. One of the ways stakeholders are identified is by interviewing the most well-connected position holders in a community, region, or, in the case of a national or international issue, socioeconomic space. These are people who routinely have contact with large numbers of people from a wide variety of subgroups and walks of life in the community. For example, religious leaders, vehicle salespeople, realtors, politicians, general store proprietors, union leaders, school principals, and major employers all get to know diverse segments of the population. The exact list of these positions should be customized to the region. In an agricultural area, the proprietor of a feed store, fertilizer store, or farm equipment dealership would be on the list. In an issue involving global finance, the list would include risk-rating agencies, stock exchanges, and the regulators of all these.

It is not necessary that these interviewees be considered stakeholders in the issue, although they could be. The point is that they know many people. They have a high level of social capital. Therefore, they are likely more able to suggest additional groups or individuals who are stakeholders.

Another social impact assessment technique that is useful is to probe interviewees about the consequences of the issue. The idea is to uncover ripple effects of the issue that may create additional rings of stakeholders. For example, the declaration of a region as an environmental preserve or protected area may have impacts on the loan portfolio at the local bank, which may have impacts on the tightening of credit available for entrepreneurial activity in the region. These unforeseen ripple effects can also be discovered by simply making lists of impacts and then asking the impacted parties what the consequences of the impacts will be for them and for others who they deal with.

Recommendations From Interviewed Stakeholders: Snowball Sampling

Once interviewing of stakeholders has started, another source of names becomes available. The stakeholders already identified can be asked who else they think is a stakeholder—that is, who else would be affected by the issue or could have an effect on the issue. This technique is known as "snowball" sampling because it increases the size of the sample as the interviewing "rolls along."[3]

The interviewing is usually limited to a fixed period. If the name of a stakeholder group is repeatedly mentioned and that group is not yet on the list, then they can be added to the list and included for interviewing toward the end of the interviewing period. If that is not possible, then at least the names of these nominated stakeholders can be listed along with the number of times they were nominated. This list can be used to improve the list of stakeholders for subsequent rounds of interviewing. The list can also help identify blind spots in the focal organization's thinking about the issue.

Determining the Boundaries of the Network

The task of listing the stakeholders to be interviewed raises the question of where to draw the boundaries of the stakeholder network. At a theoretical level, it can be argued that there are no boundaries. Everyone affects everything and is affected by everything and everyone. In practice, however, the problem is not that complicated.

The interview process has been completed when either no new names are being discovered or when those that are being discovered turn out to not care enough about the issue to be bothered with an interview. Participating in an interview takes a commitment of uncompensated time.

If that commitment seems like too much of an imposition for a named stakeholder, then the stakeholder's stake is likely negligible. The outer boundary of the stakeholder network has been reached.

Population Census Versus Survey Sample

Confusion often arises around the concept of a stakeholder network as a population as opposed to a sample from a population. When people hear the word "interview" they often presume that a survey is being conducted. Then they ask what the sample size is or should be. This shows that they do not understand the difference between a survey and a census.

A survey takes a small sample of the population and generalizes to everyone in the population. Network studies take a selected population and attempt to interview 100% of that population. Therefore, sample size is irrelevant because there is no sample. However, the percentage of the population interviewed is very relevant. Table 4.1 illustrates the point. All four rows involve doing 10 interviews. The implications for the quality of the findings are quite different depending on the population size and whether the study is a census or a sample.

Interviewing

How to Interview

Before we look at the content of the interview, it is important to consider the pros and cons of the communications channels that could be

Table 4.1. What Interviewing 10 People Means for the Quality of a Census Versus a Sample

Study type	Population size	Number of people interviewed	Percentage interviewed	Methodological evaluation
Census	10	10	100	Perfect
Census	100	10	10	Very poor
Sample	100	10	10	Excellent
Sample	1000	10	1	Very poor

used to implement the questionnaire. Every interviewing modality has its strengths and weaknesses.

Self-Complete Online Questionnaire

Self-complete online questionnaires are low cost. However, it takes more incentive to get people to complete them. It is also quite difficult to get much depth in the open-ended answers when respondents have to type out their thoughts. This modality is quite suitable for collecting rating-scale opinions from employees. It can be used with other stakeholders as well when an issue has become more heated and people are searching for a chance to have input.

Self-Complete Touch-Tone Telephone Questionnaire

A variation on the self-complete online questionnaire is the touch-tone questionnaire. With this modality, stakeholders call a toll-free telephone number and respond to questions with touch-tones. The technical name is interactive voice response (IVR) interviewing. This method has the advantage of permitting people to speak their answers to open-ended questions. In my experience, the responses are more frequent and detailed than those to web-based, open-ended questions. Another advantage is that it can be completed from any telephone, with no need for an Internet connection. It also works better for stakeholders with low levels of literacy because there is no reading involved. However, the navigation through the questionnaire takes more concentration than web question-naires. The latter are more forgiving of distractions.

Human Telephone Interview

The human telephone interview technique has the advantage of putting the initiative in the hands of the researchers. Interviewers call interviewees and either do an interview right away or make an appointment to call back later. This raises the response rate. That is a very important consideration when doing a census. The aim is always to get completed interviews with as close to 100% of the population as possible. In addition, with proper training, the human interview can be much better at eliciting richer depth of responses to open-ended questions.

The task of keeping track of complex contingencies in the flow of the interview can be automated to take the administrative burden off the interviewer and permit more attention to be devoted to probing. It is not necessary to buy professional computer-assisted telephone-interviewing software. The interview can simply use a web-based version of the questionnaire to record responses while conducting the interview in a telephone conversation.

A disadvantage that the human telephone interview shares with the previously mentioned automated interviewing techniques is the greater difficulty of establishing rapport with the interviewee, at least compared to face-to-face interviewing. For this reason, human telephone interviews are more appropriate for stakeholders who are more literate and familiar with maintaining relationships through technological channels.

Face-to-Face Interview

Face-to-face interviewing can be used with almost any stakeholder except those whose schedules or work demands make it nearly impossible to get an appointment. The technique has the same advantages as human telephone interviews in terms of better response rates. However, the greatest advantage of this technique is the superior response depth that can be achieved with the open-ended questions. Face-to-face interviews allow the establishment of much more rapport with the interviewee, which sets the stage for greater openness and willingness to expand on answers.

The face-to-face technique is also the only one that works with stakeholders who are unfamiliar or uncomfortable with private-line telephones or more sophisticated communications channels. It is the best technique in oral cultures, in remote places where animals are still used for transportation, and in places where customs require welcoming rituals before a conversation can take place. In cultures with high social distance, higher status stakeholders also require face-to-face interviewing so that the interviewer can present himself in the manner of a supplicant. Some stakeholders become insulted if treated as equals.

Advantages of Local Interviewers

Almost anyone can be trained to do the interview. However, the process will take less time if more experienced people are recruited. People with interviewing experience include marketing researchers, human resources personnel, journalists, psychologists, sociologists, anthropologists, and some kinds of professionals in health, education, and social welfare fields.

In regions where social research is seldom done, training inexperienced local interviews can add to the human capital of the community. This can be a small but a lasting benefit. Where there are educational institutions that conduct research, contracting with their personnel can make an even greater contribution to the local human capital.

Local interviewers not only have an excellent knowledge of local social customs but also know many of the stakeholders personally. This can be a tremendous advantage in actually getting the interviews done. For example, I once found myself unable to get an interview with a village council member in a South Pacific jungle community. One of the local interviewers volunteered the information that the councilor could reliably be found on Friday afternoons in a hut off a remote jungle road, drinking with his friends from a neighboring village. We cut through the foliage, and there he was, very jovial and predisposed to share all his thoughts.

In a couple of other studies, local interviewers were able to save us days of useless searching for stakeholders because they knew where and when they would all be meeting.

In another study, the leaders of a very remote village refused to talk to all outsiders except one university professor who had been working with them for decades. When that professor refused to answer our e-mails and phone calls, we were stuck. Then we came across someone who had lived in the village for a couple of months the year before. He had never done any interviewing before in his life and had little education, but said he could get in and talk to the leaders. We invested the time training him, and he got the job done.

This benefit of hiring local interviewers can be especially important when doing research in areas well outside the rule of law. Someone is always in charge, and if it happens to be a criminal or insurgent organization, local interviewers can help steer clear of dangerous people and places. Alternatively, they may have family members involved in those organizations, and they can therefore gain safe access to people and places that would otherwise be off-limits for security reasons. Security concerns are also why one seldom hears case descriptions of this advantage.

Multiple Interviews per Stakeholder Group and Multiple Groups per Stakeholder

At times it may be difficult to know who should be considered the leader of a stakeholder organization. A city council, for example, may form different coalitions on different issues. If the council is polarized on an issue, it is better to interview representatives from both sides and to not average their responses. They should be treated as two different stakeholders, both representing the council.

In other cases, there are impending elections or leadership challenges that make the current official leader appear destined for defeat. In these cases, both the incumbent and the challenger should be interviewed.

Perhaps the most difficult situation is when one hears rumors or obtains other information indicating that a leader is not accurately reflecting the opinions of the membership. When there is no challenger or opposition faction to interview for a second opinion, one must accept the current leader's legitimacy at face value. However, these suspicions should be used as hypotheses to frame ongoing monitoring of the organization's positions and the leader's support. For example, if the organization is becoming more isolated from previous allies or is losing access to resources, the hunch about the leader's lack of legitimacy with members would be supported.

The opposite type of problem sometimes occurs in small stakeholder networks where people have to shoulder multiple responsibilities. In small communities, for example, the president of the landowners' association might also be the mayor. The religious leader might also be the leaders of an environmental organization. When stakeholders wear multiple hats, it is necessary to know which hat they are wearing when being interviewed. Usually it is best to ask them which organization they think has the biggest stake and then ask them to answer as a representative of that organization only. In one study, I encountered a stakeholder who said he would need to do two separate interviews in order to represent two different stakeholder organizations. He graciously agreed to spend the time doing the interview twice. His answers in each interview were indeed distinct and consistent with the different interests of each organization.

Questions to Ask in the Interview

In order to get information that permits the development of a sound issues management strategy, there are three main types of questions that should be asked:

- Qualitative questions on issues (open-ended questions with verbal responses)
- Questions on the social license to operate (SLO) and social capital questions on the bilateral relationship between the stakeholder and focal organization (agree–disagree statements answered on ratings scales)
- Social capital questions on the multilateral relationships between the stakeholder and all the other stakeholders (rating scale evaluations of relationships)

The questions should be presented in sets. The order in which they are discussed here has worked well as a presentation order for the sets in the interview.

Qualitative Questions on Issues

The interview begins with open-ended, qualitative questions. They serve three purposes. First, they signal to the stakeholder that the interviewer is listening to them. Stakeholders get to express their hopes, fears, concerns, and opinions in their own words before all else. The fact that the interviewer listens carefully, makes notes, and asks follow-up questions shows the stakeholder that their opinions are valued. This establishes rapport that predisposes the stakeholder to complete the rest of the interview.

Second, stakeholders often do have emotionally charged opinions and concerns. They are not as likely to concentrate on the subsequent questions in the interview until they have unloaded this emotional material. Therefore, the open-ended questions at the beginning of the interview help some stakeholders concentrate better during the rest of the interview.

Third, regardless of the positioning of these questions in the interview, they elicit extremely valuable information. The answers provide the context that makes all the other responses interpretable.

The exact wording of the open-ended question can vary, but research has identified four main question topics that have been proven to build rapport and elicit valuable contextual information in many diverse cultural contexts.[4] It is a modified strengths-weaknesses-opportunities-threats (SWOT) analysis. The question topics are ordered as follows:

1. *Hopes and fears.* Talking about hopes involves assessing opportunities. Talking about fears involves facing perceived threats. The answers to these topic questions can be followed up with the probing technique known as laddering in order to uncover how their concerns connect with their values or fit into their cause and effect attributions about the situation they find themselves living in. Laddering is explained in the following section, titled "Laddering."

2. *Strengths and resources.* When asked what resources and capabilities they possess to deal with their concerns and achieve their goals, stakeholders must analyze the distance between their current situation and their hopes and fears. This impromptu gap analysis gets them thinking about their strengths, about their weaknesses, and about what a solution would look like.

3. *Barriers and obstacles.* This question topic turns attention to external impediments. The information obtained here often identifies what the stakeholder sees as the core problem for them.

4. *Plans and priorities.* To this point, stakeholders have described their current situation and anything that might be frustrating their attempts to reach their goals. This topic question solicits their ideas about what needs to change. The wording of the question should not imply who should do the changing. It is worded to elicit descriptions about what the situation would look like after the change somehow happened.

Posing an open-ended qualitative question is also a good way to end the interview. Asking for any final comments once again gives stakeholders a chance to release any emotional energy built up during the interview and communicate any deeper thinking stimulated by topics touched upon during the interview. Sometimes they are able to condense their ideas into pithy quotes.

Laddering

Laddering is an interviewing technique that was first developed in the field of marketing.[5] In the original process, consumers were first asked about the differences they noted among products. The answer to these questions usually produced a list of product features. Then the laddering began. Interviewers asked what it was about the feature that appealed to the consumer. They probed for the consequential benefits of the feature. If it was a negative feature, they probed for the benefits of avoiding the feature. Then once the benefits and consequences were established, the interviewer probed further to find out what made those important to the consumer. The answers to the latter set of probes were often values, such as family, prestige, and health.[6]

Getting to the values level often required probing techniques for bypassing conversation stoppers like "it saves money" or "it saves time." When confronted with these, the interviewer must ask why the consumer wants more time or money (e.g., "Money for what?"). The laddering process was later adapted for use with political applications and to socio-political issues.[7] In these cases, the specific product features were replaced by attributes of candidates or by complaints and issues of concern to stakeholders.

The responses to laddering probes can be graphed as an ascending means–ends hierarchy going from the most specific features to the values that make them important. Figure 4.1 provides a simplified example of a means–ends hierarchy derived from laddering interviews with a population of rural stakeholders who were experiencing a drought. The graph shows how stakeholders can go from a specific complaint or issue to the consequences (i.e., positive or negative) to the value that is either served or obstructed.

Means-ends analyses contain a hierarchical assumption that if A causes B, B does not also cause A. It is assumed that the causality is asymmetric, not symmetric. However, research has shown that that laddering data can be riddled with symmetric causality. It has been suggested that the best way to deal with this violation of the hierarchy assumption is

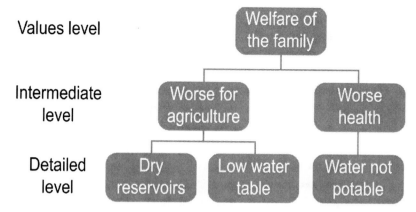

Values level

Welfare of the family

Intermediate level

Worse for agriculture

Worse health

Detailed level

Dry reservoirs

Low water table

Water not potable

Figure 4.1. A simple means–ends hierarchy derived from laddering interviews with rural stakeholders experiencing a drought.

to use network maps instead. Network maps allow concepts to be each other's causes. Networks also have the advantage of identifying which concepts are more or less central or well-connected.[8]

In 2001, I began using the network approach to mapping laddering data on stakeholder issues.[9] I was studying community stakeholders' concerns about the withdrawal of the major employer from their local economy. There were indeed some relations that fit the asymmetrical hierarchical model of causality (e.g., improved agriculture → maintain standard of living → maintain health and prevent sickness). However, there were other paths within the same data that followed the symmetrical pattern (e.g., fostering economic development → maintenance of infrastructure *and* maintenance of infrastructure → fostering economic development). Allowing both symmetric and asymmetric causality to appear where it will in the graphs increases the chances of extracting useful insights from the analysis.

Including a Bilateral Relations Section for Focal Organizations

The section of the interview with the questions that measure aspects of the relationship between the focal organization and a particular stakeholder is called the bilateral section. It is bilateral because each stakeholder is asked about only one relationship. This is to distinguish it from the multilateral section, which asks each stakeholder about his or her relations with many other stakeholders.

The bilateral section of the interview is only needed when there is a focal organization. Not all issues are focused on the activities or impacts of a single organization, project, or industry. As explained in chapter 1, stakes can be held in problems or emergent systems where there is no one organization responsible for the issue or capable or resolving the issue. In such cases, there is no focal organization; consequently, the interview does not include a bilateral section.

The bilateral section of the interview should contain the question on both the level of SLO granted and the bilateral social capital attributed to the relationship. The question format is the same. The agree–disagree questions that measure the social capital can be merged with the SLO questions.

Bilateral Questions on the SLO

The series of agree-disagree statements for measuring the SLO request that the level of agreement be indicated on a rating scale (e.g., 5 point, 7 point, or 10 point). Attempts to measure the SLO are just beginning. The field is in its infancy. The first academic conference on the topic was held at the Centre for Social Responsibility in Mining at the University of Queensland, Brisbane, in July 2011. Nonetheless, there have been some examples of successful measurement already.

Using the model developed by Ian Thomson and myself (see Figure 2.1) as a starting point, I devised a set of questions that measured withholding the license, legitimacy, acceptance, credibility, approval, trust, and identification. Because the measures are still in development, it is not possible at this point to recommend a specific wording of questions. However, question topics and some lessons that have been learned already can be shared. The SLO should address the following measures:

- *Basic personal gain.* Does the stakeholder see or anticipate any personal benefit in the operation?
- *A positive role for the operation in the wider community or region.* Does the stakeholder think the operation does or could fit into the sociopolitical ecosystem of the community or region? This

entails a range of issues from the extent and handling of the operation's negative side effects (in the language of economics, its externalities) to the perceived fairness of the operation's policies, practices, and vision for the future of the region.

- *The interpersonal trustworthiness of the operation's representatives.* Does the stakeholder believe they have displayed a willingness to reciprocate, a requisite level of mutual respect, and a level of honesty that indicates personal integrity? Does the focal organization listen and keep its promises?
- *The institutionalization of a working relationship.* Do the stakeholders collectively have a durable working relationship with the focal organization? Is the interorganizational characterized by relationship reciprocity and trust that goes above and beyond the occasional errors or misdeeds by individual members of either organization?

The original questions we used to measure withholding an SLO did not work very well because they were negatively worded. Therefore, people who granted an SLO had to disagree with them in order to indicate a positive attitude. About half of the interviewees got mixed up. The interviews slowed down because of the double negative. Therefore, it was decided that the measure of withholding or withdrawing an SLO should simply be the absence of positive ratings for positively worded questions.

Not all the results were completely as predicted by the Thomson and Boutilier model. The prototype agree–disagree statements were presented to stakeholders of two different mining operations in two different Latin American countries. One was an operating mine that had established local relationships for 15 years. The other was an exploration project in the feasibility stage that had only been developing relationships for about three years.

The questions worked well in terms of gauging the general sociopolitical support for the project. The responses were averaged, and arbitrary scores were chosen to indicate boundaries between the levels of SLO (see Figure 2.1). Nevertheless, there was disconcerting disconnect between the findings and the theory. The theory predicts that the levels would be ordered so that a person could not skip a level. For example, someone who granted an acceptance level of license but withheld an approval level should not strongly agree with the statements about identification with the project or the industry. In reality, however, many people did skip levels, especially at the exploration project. The questions did the job of measuring overall acceptance levels, but they did not have the steplike response characteristics predicted by the theory.

There are several possible explanations for this. One is that the statements to measure the highest level, identification, were interpreted differently by people who did not have long relationships with the focal organization. In the absence of sufficient interaction to be able to answer the question, they may have fabricated an answer by (a) giving the company the benefit of the doubt, (b) answering in terms of how they hoped the relationship would turn out, or (c) answering in terms how they thought other people would answer. If this were the case, some measure of how well the parties in the relationship know each other might be needed in order to weight the statements. If a stakeholder has not yet gotten to know the focal organization very well, then questions that presume a deeper knowledge could be discounted. Another solution might be to develop distinctly different sets of questions for different stages of a relationship.

Another possible explanation for the level-skipping phenomenon might be that the highest level of SLO is not an individual-level phenomenon. It could be a community act or a social consensus that emerges out of repeated interactions. Perhaps interactions between organizations are more important at this level. If so, the proper way to measure the identification level would be to look for characteristics of the community's joint activities and interaction patterns with the focal organizations. The measures would have to be at the community level, not at the individual level.

This explanation could be generalized to other levels of SLO as well. Perhaps the whole phenomenon of an SLO is a group-level phenomenon. Indeed a very preliminary analysis did suggest that the expected steplike pattern through the stages was more evident when group means were used rather individual means. However, more analysis on a larger set of data would be needed to know at what level, under what circumstances, and in which aspects the SLO is a group-level phenomenon.

There may be other possibilities as well, including the possibility that the cumulative assumption in the Thomson and Boutilier model must be modified. Future research will undoubtedly sort out these questions.

Bilateral Questions on Social Capital in the Relationship

If there is a focal organization in the issue, then it is a good idea to have a close look at the social capital that each stakeholder perceives to exist in his or her relationship with that stakeholder. As suggested in chapter 3, the definition of social capital proposed by Janine Nahapiet and Sumatra Ghoshal not only captures the noncircular core of concept but also provides a practical foundation for measuring social capital. Nahapiet and Ghoshal proposed a three-dimensional view of social capital. The structural dimension is given by the network structure. The relational dimension deals with the affective elements of the relationship. The cognitive dimension is about shared cognitive frameworks such as languages, analytic paradigms, and goals for the future.

Nahapiet and Ghoshal's structural dimension is best measured by looking at the whole network map and the stakeholder's specific place in it. These would be measures such as the stakeholder's centrality, the stakeholder's opportunities to act as a bridge across structural holes, and the stakeholder's portfolio of strong and weak ties in the network. It is also possible to measure the structural elements of individual relationships, such as the frequency of contact. However, experience has shown these relationship-level measures of structure to be idiosyncratic. That is, they are determined by quirky accidents of proximity and routine. They do not have much bearing on the aspects of the relationship that affect issues management strategy. Instead of adding to the understanding of sociopolitical dynamics, these measures only add noise.

The relational dimension of social capital can be measured at the level of bilateral relationships with just two questions related to trust and reciprocity. The words in brackets should be changed to proper names as appropriate. The questions are introduced in the usual way for the agree–disagree format. The points of the rating scale are explained, and then the statement is posed (e.g., "How much do you agree or disagree with the following statement?"):

- "The focal organization keeps its promises to us," or "The focal organization fulfills its commitments to us."
- "The focal organization listens to us."

The cognitive dimension can be measured with one question, but it should be customized to the situation in order to focus on the most relevant shared cognitive construction:

- "Our organization agrees [we agree] with [the focal organization] on goals for the future," or "Our organization and [the focal organization] share the same understanding of the problem we face with [name of problem or issue]," or "Our organization and [the focal organization] use the same [approach or methods or framework] for dealing with [name of problem or issue]."

The measures of bilateral social capital show how much collaborative capacity there is in a relationship. However, that capacity will not be used if there is no motivation to use it. Therefore, it is also a good idea to measure the motivation to collaborate. This can be done with the following question:

- "We need the collaboration of [the focal organization] to reach our most important goals."

Measures of Multilateral Social Capital

The multilateral social capital section of the interview is necessary for a network approach to issues management. This is where stakeholders are asked about the level of social capital in their relationships with each other. For well-connected stakeholders, this can involve dozens of relationships. For that reason, the questions about each relationship have to be few and short.

In collaboration with the Australian Centre for Corporate Social Responsibility,[10] we found a way to condense the relational social capital questions down to one item. Factor analyses on proprietary data with several measures of the relational dimension showed that the core of the relational dimension could be measured by asking for ratings of the degree of satisfaction with the relationship with the other stakeholder in question. Therefore, it takes only two quick questions to measure the social capital a stakeholder has in each relationship. First, the stakeholder is asked if they have a relationship with a given stakeholder (prelisted or named by the interviewee). If so, then they are asked the following questions:

- "How satisfied are you with your relationship with [stakeholder name]?"
- "On matters of mutual concern, to what extent do you agree on goals for the future?"

During the interview, stakeholders make these multilateral social capital ratings in response to lists of other stakeholder that are presented to them. Methods for developing such lists were described earlier in this chapter. It is easier for the interviewee if the stakeholders are grouped in related categories that interviewees themselves are likely to use (e.g., all the government bodies and agencies, all the stakeholders from a specific village, all the private companies, or all the environmental groups).

After these prelisted ratings are done, interviewees are in a good position to suggest additional stakeholders that may not have been listed. This is how the snowball sampling progresses. If there is time, it is also desirable to have the interviewee rate their social capital with these additional nominated stakeholders. Alternatively, the nominees can simply be listed in the final report. In any case, for the snowball sampling, these nominees would immediately be sought for interviews if they were mentioned by more than one or two interviewees.

Questions for Managers

This chapter covered the technical side of getting good information on what is going on in your stakeholder network. Having clear answers to the following questions will help you make the various decisions that you confront when trying to collect good information:

- Which of your staff and your stakeholders have a lot of contact with a wide variety of people? Who do they think the stakeholders are, and why?
- Are there stakeholders who know much more about all the elaborate aspects of an issue than others? Are they leading

groups, or are they individuals? Do others respect their opinions and use them as a sounding board?

- Do stakeholders disagree on what the most important issue is? Do you have interviews with all the dissenting view holders?

- Do you have any contextual evidence that any of the stakeholder group leaders does not articulate the attitudes of the group he or she represents? Are there any whose leadership is being openly challenged? Have you interviewed the challengers or dissenters?

- If you have interviewed representatives of local government, how could you find out if there are there sharp differences of opinion corresponding to political parties or alliances? If there are such divisions, have you interviewed representatives from all sides?

CHAPTER 5

Summarizing the Data

In this chapter we examine the processes used to condense questionnaire data into summaries that provide a basic view of what the issues are and which stakeholders are concerned about them. The steps described in chapter 5 provide the building blocks for the strategic analyses described in chapter 6.

Analysis of Qualitative Issue Data

Qualitative data give context to the quantitative data. For example, they can explain why all the taxi drivers are opposed to a new public transit plan. They can explain why the shop owners and the teachers in a community are tightly connected into a high social capital network. However, the qualitative data can be slippery without some kind of organizing framework. The quickest and easiest way to organize qualitative data is to put them into categorical boxes and then count how many there are in each box.

Categorizing Comments About Issues

The qualitative questions in the interview described previously will generate comments made by stakeholders. The comments are the basic level of data. Each one is unique. However, there are many similarities among them, and these can be used as the basis for creating categories. For example, one person's comments may take the form of a little story about how annoying it is to have to clean a fresh layer of dust off the household furniture daily. Another might come right to point and say there is too much dust coming from the gravel pit at the edge of town. Both of these share the similarity of claiming that there is too much dust. The researcher then could define a comment category labeled "too much dust." In addition to the verbal label, the researcher would give it an arbitrary numeric label (e.g., 01–02–08). Reading through all the comments, the researcher would make notes beside every stakeholder's name about which categories of comments they made. For example, the researcher might have a spreadsheet row for stakeholder 038 with cells to the right of the stakeholders' name (or identification number) showing that the person mentioned comments 01–02–08, 01–03–02, and 05–03–01.

From here it is easy to count the frequencies of mentions of each code. Moreover, the counts can be done within categories of stakeholders in order to make it possible to arrive at statements like "The stakeholders who withheld a social license to operate (SLO) complained about too much dust at a rate of 0.80 mentions per capita whereas the stakeholders granted an approval level of social license to operate (SLO) only mentioned too much dust 0.12 times per capita." The per capita mention rate is simply the number of mentions of the category by group members divided by the number of group members. Even if there are different numbers of stakeholders in each subgrouping of stakeholders, their qualitative responses can be compared in a numeric way.

Multiple Levels of Categories

The most difficult part about counting qualitative categories of comments is the creation of the categories. The best way to start is to try to create intermediate categories that capture repeated themes. By the end of the first reading, the researcher usually wants to go back and either merge some categories or make even finer distinctions.

The best way to handle this process is to create three levels of categories. The researcher might identify 150 to 200 detailed-level categories that all fit into 45 to 75 intermediate-level categories. Those, in turn, all belong to anywhere from 5 to 10 global-level categories. Typical global categories are things like environmental concerns, economic concerns, social problems, communication and relationship issues, infrastructure needs, and government and legal issues.

Having multiple levels of coding categories lets the researcher make statements like "The shop owners mentioned 'social problems' more than other groups of stakeholders, and within the global category of social problems, their most frequently mentioned intermediate level concerns were 'vandalism/graffiti,' 'youth crime,' and 'youth drug use.'"

The aim of the coding stage of qualitative analysis is to have a matrix with a row for each stakeholder containing a list of all the categories used by that stakeholder at all three levels of coding specificity. Spreadsheets can be programmed to automatically sum the more detailed codes into the higher-level codes to which they belong.

The process of developing a good three-layer-coding framework requires a lot of modification of previous categories. This, in turn, requires going back and recoding the comments that were coded before the change. It is typical for a researcher to read all the comments at least three times and a subset of comments many more times. It is time-consuming work, but so far there are no shortcuts. Automatic text analysis software has not yet advanced to the level where it saves time. To date, the software still adds more work than it saves, unless of course, one is going to ana-lyze thousands of stakeholder comments or one is going to collect data repeatedly across time on the same set of questions and issues.

There are some decisions that have to be made in the coding pro-cess. Often there are stakeholders who repeat themselves. They go on and on about a single detailed idea and therefore generate a mountain of mentions for that category. Should the verbal habits of one such person be allowed to make that category more important than the categories mentioned by people who simply say what they mean once and then move on? If one prefers to avoid the kind of distortion a verbose person can create in the data, then one simply institutes a coding rule that only allows one mention of a detailed code per interview. Under such a rule, a stakeholder's repeat mentions of the same category are just not counted.

A no-repeat-code-use rule applied at the detailed level of codes does not prevent a person from mentioning several aspects of an issue that all have different detailed codes. For example, a stakeholder might make comments that falls into a set of categories like "graffiti," "vandalism," "lack of youth recreation facilities," "shoplifting teens," "street racing youth," and "youth drug use." These might all get counted under an intermediate category called "youth problems." By using all these detailed categories, a single stakeholder could raise the frequency of mention for "youth problems." Is this desirable?

The researcher has to decide at this point what they want the data to emphasize. If a no-repeat-code-use rule were applied at the intermediate code level, the data would count stakeholders' concerns about intermediate level issues on the basis of one stakeholder, one vote. By contrast, if multiple detailed codes were allowed to raise the frequencies for intermediate codes, the data would give a better indication of the extent to which stakeholders had elaborated views on an intermediate level issue. Elaborated views usually indicate more depth of concern and more motivation to act on the issue. Both perspectives are valuable. The researcher might have the luxury of enough time to do both in order to extract the insights each offers.

Another decision that has to be made in the development of a three-tiered coding frame is when and where to use categories of categories. Particularly at the detailed and intermediate levels, it is desirable to label the categories so that you can later distinguish which ones contained negative or unfavorable comments and which ones contained positive or supportive comments. It is also often useful to have additional categories of categories like (a) suggestions for action, (b) perceptions of the situation, and (c) personally experienced impacts. The problem is that not all issues will generate all these categories of categories. If one tries to create a matrix containing all the possibilities, many cells will be empty, and it will become much harder to classify comments that have elements of all the classification attributes used to generate the matrix. Therefore, these additional categorical distinctions are best used selectively when you notice that a particular topic has produced many comments that could be classified along these lines.

Which Issue Categories Connect With Which Stakeholders

Once the frequency matrix of stakeholders and their coded mentions is ready, it can be pasted or imported into a network graphing program to generate a map of which stakeholders mentioned which comments and how many times. The typical graph of all such connections is too full of links to be interpretable. There are many tactics that can be used to simplify the graph. Each one has the potential to reveal a different insight. For example, one can look at one category of stakeholders at a time. One can look at only the stakeholder-to-issue links that were mentioned more frequently. One can look at each global issue category one by one. Each of these views of the data reveals something that argues for one strategic issues management direction or against another.

Figure 5.1 shows the issues as squares and the stakeholders as circles. It is called a "two-mode" graph because it contains two different types of entities: issues and stakeholders. Some of the issues were mentioned by more than one stakeholder (e.g., issues A, C, and D). The strategic implication is that issue B, therefore, is a relatively idiosyncratic concern of only stakeholder 5. The graph also shows that some stakeholders mentioned multiple issues (e.g., stakeholder 5). The strategic implication is that stakeholder 5 was probably more well-informed about the concerns of all stakeholders.

The visual interpretability of the approach depicted in Figure 5.1 is both its great strength and its great weakness. The limitation of the two-mode network graphs is the need for simplicity. The numbers of issues, stakeholders, and ties among them are usually much greater than shown in Figure 5.1. In order to make the graph useful, it must be simplified.

One way to simplify the graph is to include only those stakeholders who made multiple mentions of an intermediate or global issue. This automatically excludes detailed-level issues from the graph. It shows only those ties with higher frequencies of mention in a dataset where multiple detailed codes were allowed to raise intermediate code frequencies. By

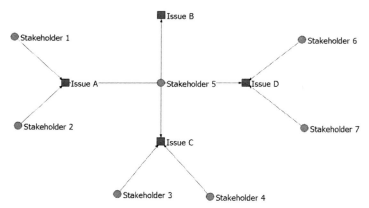

Figure 5.1. A two-mode network graph showing the stakeholders (circles) who mentioned more aspects (detailed codes) of each intermediate issue (squares).

permitting only higher numbers of mentions to be included the graph tends to show only those stakeholders who had more elaborated opinions on each of the issues. They are more likely promoters of, or experts on, the issue they are connected to.

There are strategic insights to be gained from this two-mode view of the data. However, the simplification also hides many details that are useful for developing more detailed strategic plans. In the next chapter we look at techniques that take account of most details.

Issue Networks Based on Comentions

Another way to get insights out of qualitative data is to reduce the network so that it only shows issue codes and ignores who mentioned them. Technically this is known as going from a two-mode network (i.e., stakeholders and issues) to a one-mode network (i.e., just issues). Most network graphic software does this automatically. The advantage is that it shows which issues were mentioned together by stakeholders. For example, if 90% of the stakeholders who mentioned the environment also mentioned health, then there would be an extremely strong tie between these two issues in the graph. In a manner of speaking, the graph shows how the issues are linked in the collective mind of the stakeholders.

Figure 5.2 shows a one-mode network of issues that were mentioned together in interviews with stakeholders. The sizes of the circles reflect betweenness centrality and their vertical positions reflect eigenvector centrality. Dust and traffic are high in both kinds of centrality. The triad of jobs, training, and higher incomes is located higher than the crime and inflation pair because the triad is interconnected. With more connections each, they have more eigenvector centrality.

Figure 5.2 is an invented example typical of the kinds of issues that arise when a large job-creating project commences construction in a small town without any other large employers. During the construction phase, the prime concerns are annoyances caused by things like dust and truck traffic. Some people see these as worth it because they will be accompanied by economic advantages like jobs, training, and higher incomes. Other people focus primarily on the loss of their quiet, uneventful way of life. They assert that newcomers will either bring crime or that the higher wages will only mean higher prices and therefore a lower standard of living.

From a strategic perspective, Figure 5.2 suggests that traffic and dust are linked in people's minds. This suggests that the researcher should ask why. Are the roads paved? If not, is the truck traffic raising dust? If so, the top issues management strategy would be to implement measure that would keep the dust down. The best method might be spreading water or tar on the surface. Alternatively, it might be paving the sections most exposed to wind. Whatever the technical solution, the issue has created a sociopolitical risk that could leave a negative legacy if not reduced.

The other strategic insight that Figure 5.2 suggests is that some people see themselves as future employees or suppliers to either company or the prosperous workers. Others, however, see themselves as likely to be left behind. This should prompt further questions about the characteristics of those who fear not benefiting from the economic development. With that kind of profile, it should be possible to envision community development initiatives that minimize the number of nonbenefiters and the gap between benefiters and nonbenefiters. Such initiatives would ideally be undertaken in partnership with local government and community groups.

Issue Networks Based on Attributed Consequences

For researchers who have time to read the open-ended responses yet another time, the links among issues can be coded to represent one issue

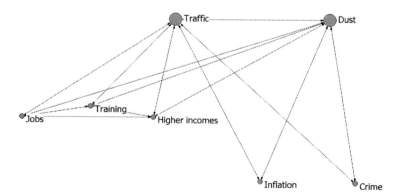

Figure 5.2. Network of issues based on how often they were mentioned together.

being a consequence of another. In the section of chapter 4 titled "Questions to Ask in the Interview," we examined the how the interviewing techniques known as laddering could produce qualitative responses linked to each other by hierarchical relations describing means-and-ends and cause-and-effect relations. We noted that the most realistic representations of stakeholders' concerns and issues use network graphs in order to allow for both reciprocal causality and one-way means–ends relations. For brevity, we refer to both causality-based and means-ends–based attributions as "consequence" attributions.

When a stakeholder is responding to the laddering questions and implies that A is a consequence of B, then a special tie can be noted between these codes. The more stakeholders who make the same causal link, the more one begins to see the emergence of the stakeholders' collective view of the situation's dynamics. This kind of insight is invaluable in many areas of issues management. It can reveal places where stakeholders fail to see a connection that really exists or what they are ready to accept as a top priority even before they have met to talk about it. This kind of data can create multicausal graphs that will be hierarchical to the exact extent that stakeholders collectively hold hierarchical views.

Figures 5.3 and 5.4 show consequential links attributed by stakeholders between pairs of ideas (i.e., impacts, issues, suggestions, and values). It is a fictitious example that incorporates insights from several cases in which communities faced a change in their fundamental character. In this case, a farming community in a very arid region faces a proposal for a dam on a nearby river flowing through a deep gorge. The dam will increase the total amount of productive farmland available in the region. Those who would lose some land will end up with a little more than others, but everyone will get more land for productive use. Moreover, the project and the infrastructure that would come with it promise to create some spin-off economic activity that would diversify the regional economy and nearly double the local population.

The example supposes that stakeholders were first asked what changes they anticipated as a result of the dam. For this reason "building the dam" is the base issue in both figures. Then, applying the laddering technique, it is further supposed that they were asked why these changes are important to them. Typically the answers in cases like this fall into four main categories:

1. Impacts, either experienced, hoped for, or feared
2. Values, either promoted or inhibited by the impact noted (e.g., environmental preservation)
3. Proposals for dealing with the issue (e.g., more communication or more regulation)
4. Continued listing of issues, ignoring the request for explanations of what makes the issue important

Figures 5.3 and 5.4 illustrate how the links observed in open-ended verbal answers could be consequential attributions in any of the following ways:

1. *Causal.* Idea A leads to idea B (e.g., "more agricultural irrigation" leads to "more agricultural land/production").
2. *Means and Ends.* Idea A is an instance or manifestation of idea B, which is seen as a more general concept or an overarching value (e.g., airborne dust is an example of a risk to the higher value of health). See Figure 4.1 for an illustration.
3. *Proscriptive.* Idea A means we must implement idea B (e.g., "community mistrust" means we "need more public education").

Figures 5.3 and 5.4 show links that met a criterion of having been mentioned by a minimum number of people. In general, links mentioned by only one or two people can be deleted. To simplify visual interpretation of the graphs, consequences that were seldom linked to further consequences or values were placed at the bottom-right area. In general, the impacts tend to appear at the bottom and the proscriptions tend to appear at the top. The vertical position of the issues is set manually by comparing how many arrows they have leading into them. Those receiving more arrows are placed higher.

The sizes of the circles in these graphs were based on the eigenvector centrality of the issues. In both graphs, there were relatively high centrality issues at the middle level of height in the graph. It is common for such intermediate level issues to have a pivotal character. They should be examined closely to see if they represent the most disputed framing of the controversy.

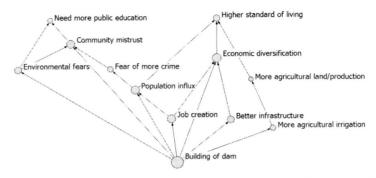

Figure 5.3. Consequential links among issues in the collective mind of supporters in a fictitious dam in an arid agricultural area.

Figure 5.3 contains an illustration the pivotal nature of the middle-level issues on these types of graphs. In the view of the supporters of the dam, the consequence labeled "economic diversification" is a key justification for the project. It has a higher level of eigenvector centrality because several divergent branches of reasoning converge on it (e.g., "building of dam," "job creation," and "better infrastructure"), and it points to a more well-connected further justification (i.e., "higher standard of living"). Another pivotal medium-level issue is "population influx." The supporters see it as a positive consequence leading to a higher standard of living. They acknowledge, however, that it raises the fear of increased crime in some stakeholders' minds. However, the supporters view the community

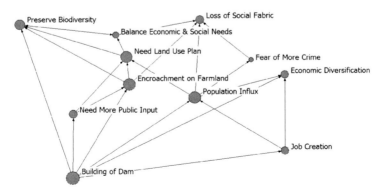

Figure 5.4. Consequential links among issues in the collective mind of opponents in a fictitious dam in an arid agricultural area.

mistrust as a fear-based phenomenon that can be eliminated with a strong dose of the facts ("need more public education").

Figure 5.4 shows a different framing of the community concerns. The opponents of the project acknowledge the job creation and economic diversification, but they are more likely to see its undesirable consequences if it is not done with community input. For them, the economic development will change the character of the community. That could easily result in a "loss of social fabric" and problems with the use and allocation of land for various purposes and priorities. Without a plan and community input into its formulation, they believe the community could lose social capital and environmental biodiversity.

There are double-headed arrows in Figure 5.4 among "preserve biodiversity," "balance economic and social needs," and "loss of social fabric." Double-headed arrows mean that many people mentioned one of them as the reason that the other was important. For example, those who were explaining why they thought that economic and social needs should be balanced said a balance was important in order to avoid a loss of social fabric or of biodiversity. Likewise, many who said it was important to preserve the social fabric or the biodiversity justified their answers by saying it is important to balance social and economic needs. The strategic implication for issues managers is that these three consequences are powerful justifications for the opponents. They have the power of values in terms of framing and reframing issues.

If a medium-level issue can be rewired or reframed to be seen as an exemplar of one of higher-level value or consequence, it will be more accepted. For example, if economic diversification were framed as a factor contributing to the preservation of the social fabric through its ability to provide jobs for youth who would otherwise leave the region to find opportunities in the city, then economic diversification would be seen in much more positive light by opponents and by the undecided who share the opponents' values. Likewise, if "population influx" were reframed as "population preservation" by virtue of the increased opportunities that would be available to locals, then it, too, would be viewed more as a positive consequence of the building of the dam.

Reframing intermediate-level consequences is usually a more effective issues management strategy than throwing more facts at public presumed to be fearful or ignorant. The research and analysis that go into producing a map of the consequence hierarchies among issues and concerns provides the level of detail needed to understand which issues are pivotal and which can be framed to align with the values that opponents or undecided stakeholders already hold.

Scoring Perceptions of the Bilateral Relationship

The next section of the interview after the open-ended questions is a good place to ask about the bilateral relationships between the interviewee's organization and the focal company. This section usually contains questions that measure the SLO, which include a subset of questions for measuring the social capital in the relationship. This section can also contain any custom questions about the relationship that may be of interest.

To score the bilateral social capital questions, average the "listens to us" ratings with the "keeps promises" ratings to produce the subscore for Nahapiet and Ghoshal's relational dimension (see the section of chapter 4 titled, "Bilateral Questions on Social Capital in the Relationship"). Use Nahapiet and Ghoshal's cognitive question (e.g., "agree on goals for the future") as the subscore for the cognitive dimension. Then average the relational subscore with the cognitive subscore. This produces a social capital score for the relationship between every stakeholder and the focal organization. If a stakeholder does not answer one of the questions, do not count it as a rating of zero. Count it as missing data. If it were counted as a score of zero, it would bring down the social capital score artificially.

To score the SLO, average all the questions used to measure it. Again, do not treat missing data as ratings of zero. Some day it will be possible to create subscale scores for the theoretical components of the SLO (i.e., legitimacy, acceptance, credibility, approval, trust, and identification). As of yet, however, these are not ready. Instead, levels of SLO granted can be defined by creating arbitrary boundaries in the scale. For example, if a 5-point scale were used, the boundaries might look like the following:

- Withheld or withdrawn: scores from 1 to less than 2.75
- Acceptance:
  - Low: scores from 2.75 to less than 3.25
  - High: scores from 3.25 to less than 3.75

- Approval: scores from 3.75 to less than 4.25
- Identification: scores from 4.25 to 5.0.

Acceptance is the most commonly granted level of SLO. Sometimes so many stakeholders fall into that SLO score range that it is helpful to distinguish among those in the lower half (i.e., low acceptance) and those in the upper half (high acceptance).

The exact boundary points must be calibrated in each study. Experience shows that they seem to vary by the culture's generalized trust level. Lower trust cultures will need lower boundary points.[1] Other factors that can help in the calibration are signs of the SLO collectively produced at the community level. For example, the town of Sudbury, Ontario, Canada, constructed a 9-meter-high five-cent piece (i.e., a nickel) as a symbol of the town's identity and as a tourist attraction.[2] If one were deciding on where to put the top boundary on the SLO scale for the nickel industry in Sudbury, this collective symbol would prompt one to set it high because so many people would likely grant high SLO levels that the data would need more dissection at the top end than at the bottom end. At the other end of the scale, the area around Rio Blanco in northern Peru made headlines in 2009 when 15 to 20 unidentified armed locals invaded the mine owned by Zijin Mining Group, overpowered security guards, and killed two workers. Several others are still missing and no one has been charged. An assessment of the mining company's SLO in this region would need finer distinctions at the lower end of the scale.

The measures of social capital and SLO provide strategically useful criteria for creating subgroupings of stakeholders. For example, one could compare the high-SLO granters versus the low-SLO granters on the per capita frequency of mentioning various issues. High versus low categories on social capital and the SLO can also be combined with other classifications of stakeholders. For example, one could examine the relative frequency of high–social capital relations with the focal organization among stakeholder categories like businesses, government, environmental groups, and community groups. The results would indicate which ones are most likely to collaborate with the focal organization on an initiative.

Analysis of Stakeholder Network Data

Preparing the Data to be Graphed

The analysis of the multilateral social capital data is the essence of developing strategic insights from stakeholder networks. All of chapter 5 deals with how to do this. At this point we simply deal with how to get the data ready for graphing.

The multilateral section of the interview produces two ratings on every relationship that the stakeholder has (see the section of chapter 4 titled "Measures of Multilateral Social Capital"). To get the level of social capital in the relationship, average these two ratings.

The ratings produce a matrix in which the rows are the stakeholders making the ratings, and the columns are the other parties to each relationship. The matrix must be square; therefore, the names of the stakeholders in the rows have to be the same as those of the stakeholders in the columns. If an interviewed stakeholder rates a relationship with a stakeholder that was not interviewed and not listed on the interview questionnaire, then a new column has to be created to contain that rating *and* a new row has to be created for that rated stakeholder in order to keep the matrix square.

Once the square matrix of ratings is done, it can be imported into any number of network graphing software packages. For many years during the infancy of the social network analysis field, the only available software packages were developed at universities. Two of the earliest packages that continue to be widely used, continually improved, and well supported with documentation and training are UCINET and Payek. The website of the International Network for Social Network Analysis[3] has a page listing many free or free-trial software packages for social network graphing. There are dozens of commercially available packages as well. Some of them produce impressive graphics from an intuitive interface that beginners can learn quickly.

Network Graph Basics

Lines as Relationships

The circles represent stakeholder organizations. The lines between the circles represent relations of social capital between the organizations. These relations are estimated from the ratings attributed to them by the interviewees. The ratings were made on a scale of one to five as described in the section of chapter 4 titled "Measures of Multilateral Social Capital."

It is possible to represent the strength of the relationships by showing them as lines of different thickness. Some graphing packages also allow the relationship-strength numbers to be shown beside the line. However, both of these create visual clutter when there are more than a dozen stakeholders. An alternative that produces graphs that are easier to interpret at a glance is to delete all the lines that represent the weaker relationships. Showing only the strongest relationships makes it possible to quickly see which stakeholders have the greatest potential for mutual collaboration. Then different graphs can be produced to show only the weakest relationships or relationships above or below a given level of strength.

The lines could represent the ratings attributed to the relationship by either one or both of the two parties to the relationship. If both were interviewed, their perceptions can be blended by averaging their ratings. In the case where one party rated a relationship with a stakeholder who was not interviewed, the social capital score for the relationship is based only on the perceptions of the party that was interviewed. The same happens when one party mentions the relationship but the other does not reciprocally mention it. These cases can be distinguished by making the lines between the circles into arrows. That is, the arrowhead at one end of the line indicates which stakeholder was the perceiver and which was the perceived. Lines with arrowheads at both ends represent relationships mentioned by both parties.

Colors and Sizes of Circles as Stakeholder Attributes

With most packages there is also an option to include data on the characteristics of each stakeholder. These could be things like the level of support the stakeholder expresses for the project, a code for the issue of greatest concern to the stakeholder, or the socioeconomic sector of the organization the stakeholder represents (e.g., government, business, and civic sector). These stakeholder attributes can be very useful in coloring the stakeholders' circle on the graph. For example, you can assign a different color to each category of stakeholders. This would let you see, for example, if the environmental groups are bonded or not, if the government organizations have a central coordinating body, or if the agricultural groups have any communication at all with the tourism groups.

For stakeholder attributes that are continuous, rather than categorical, you can select the colors so that they cover a range of the spectrum. However, this can make finer distinctions difficult to detect visually. Another option is to represent continuous attributes by the size of the circles. For example, the level of SLO granted by each stakeholder is a continuous variable ranging from 1 to 5. You can set a minimum circle size to represent 1 and a maximum to indicate 5. Then the sizes of the circles will automatically reflect the level of SLO granted. This lets you see, for example, if the SLO withholders are tightly connected with one another or are dispersed throughout the network in an unorganized way.

Positions of Circles as Stakeholder Attributes

The positions of the circles can signify various things depending on the type of graph. If you wish to see the relationships maintained by a single stakeholder group, you can put it at the center and then define concentric rings around it in which you can place other stakeholders with whom the focal organization has varying strengths of relationships. The strongest relationship partners would be in the innermost ring. Those in the outermost ring would be stakeholders with whom the focal organization has the weakest relationships.

Grouping stakeholders by geography can sometimes be informative. In one study, we had stakeholders from all parts of a state in a developed country. After grouping the stakeholders in clusters that more or less corresponded to their geographical region, we noted that those in one particular region had many more relationships among themselves than the others. To take this approach to a higher level, the longitude and latitude of the stakeholders' locations can be included as two of their attributes. Some graphing software packages will then permit these to be used as positioning coordinates. Of course, the raw longitude and latitude data may have to be transformed to conform to the graphing plane, but a little ingenuity can reproduce the geographic positions.

The position on the graph can also be used to represent how influential the stakeholder group is with other stakeholders. Sociological research shows that an actor's influence is highly associated with the centrality of the actor in the network.[4] The next section looks at how two different measures of the centrality of the actor in the network can be simultaneously displayed using a combination of circle size and position.

How Graphs Show Power Differences Among Stakeholders

There are two types of actor centrality in networks that have been associated with the level of power and influence a network member enjoys.[5] Eigenvector centrality (sometimes called "eigenvalue centrality") indicates how well connected each stakeholder is to well-connected others. It corresponds roughly to being at the center of a bonded cluster in a network (e.g., the committee/tribe structure in Figure 3.3).

Betweenness centrality measures the number of times a circle on a network graph appears in the shortest path between pairs of circles. Betweenness centrality can be thought of in terms of messages flowing among all stakeholders in the network. Some messages will be relayed through shorter paths. Some stakeholders will be on the shortest paths more often than others. They are the ones with high betweenness centrality. Stakeholders with high bridging social capital have high betweenness centrality because messages flowing from one bonded group to another all have to pass through the bridging stakeholder, no matter which members originate or receive them (e.g., the core elements of the silos/factions structure in Figure 3.3).

Stakeholders can have both high eigenvector and high betweenness centrality. For example, stakeholders forming the hubs of hub-and-spokes structures (e.g., the absolute dictatorship and exclusive elite structures in Figure 3.3) enjoy both high betweenness centrality and high eigenvector centrality relative to others in the network.

Because both types of centrality are important indicators of influence in a network, we would like to see them both represented visually at the same time. To do this, one can be represented by position and the other by the size of the circle. Eigenvector centrality is most easily represented by position. For example, in the NetDraw software attached to the UCINET package, the principle components button automatically arranges the circles according to their eigenvector centrality. A simple rotation of an eigenvector centrality graph can place the most influential stakeholders at the top and the least influential at the bottom. This offers a visually intuitive portrayal of the pecking order in the network. Then betweenness centrality can be calculated with a few clicks and applied to determine the size of the circles. Figure 5.5 illustrates how both eigenvector and betweenness centralities can vary separately. In the top panel, the sizes of the circles have been adjusted to reflect the betweenness centrality of the circles. The bottom panel shows the same graph with the eigenvector centrality of the circles represented by their vertical positions. Note that stakeholder F is high on both eigenvector and betweenness centrality. Stakeholder D is high on eigenvector centrality but relatively low on

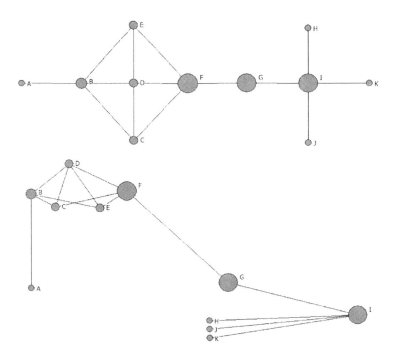

Figure 5.5. A stakeholder network illustrating the difference between eigenvector centrality and betweenness centrality.

betweenness. By contrast, stakeholder I is low on eigenvector centrality but high on betweenness centrality.

How to Identify Separate Groups, Cliques, and Clusters

Rational Categorization

The rational approach involves categorizing stakeholders according to predefined attributes that they share. For example, these could include the following:

- Industry (e.g., agriculture, transportation, manufacturing, local government)
- Economic sector (e.g., private, public, and civic or voluntary)
- Size (e.g., number of employees or members)
- Geographic range or proximity (i.e., local, regional, national, or international)

A disadvantage of rationally derived clusters is that they may contain so many diverse stakeholders that it is difficult to address them as a group. They may not have relationships among each other. In terms of developing communications strategies, this implies that they should be brought together in order to form a body coherent enough to speak with one voice. For example, a category like "small business" could contain many family-run operations that have never had any contact with one another. If, however, a neighborhood or regional business association were created, they could articulate a position that would have more sociopolitical legitimacy than the average of their separate opinions from a random sample opinion survey.

Single-Variable Groupings by Range or Category

Whereas the rational approach generally uses group demographic characteristics, the same kind of analysis can be performed on a variable that comes from responses to interview questions. For example, one might divide the SLO scores into the four levels shown in Figure 2.1. Then the groups could be compared in terms of their other characteristics like industry sector, geographic area, empirical cluster membership, and so forth. These comparisons can lead to strategic ideas for raising the level of SLO or for communications initiatives aimed at reframing issues.

Empirical Clusters of Stakeholders

The bottom panel of Figure 5.5 shows how the network divides itself into the cluster of stakeholders on the top left (i.e., A to F) and the cluster on the bottom left (i.e., G to K). This is an empirical grouping of stakeholders. It reflects the naturally observed relationships among them. This type of clustering of stakeholders has the great advantage of reflecting reality as it was when the interviews were done. Moreover, because relationships tend to endure across months and years, it probably reflects reality for a good period after the interviews.

Grouping stakeholders in this way require some caution. Sometimes the grouping is based on a narrow aspect of social capital. Care must be taken not to confuse it with a high capacity for collaboration. For example, media outlets often have relationships with many stakeholders and therefore have high eigenvector centrality. In a graph like the bottom panel of Figure 5.5, they would appear to lead a separate cluster of stakeholders. However, because their relationships are based purely in information exchange, their cluster is not necessarily capable of collaborating among themselves.

There are many other empirical methods for finding natural clusters of stakeholders in a network.[6] For example, one can calculate how much each stakeholder's contacts contribute to holding the network together. Then by deleting each of these successively from the network, the resulting subgroups can be defined. As more stakeholders are deleted, the network breaks into more distinct subgroups. The demographic and attitudinal profiles of these groups can then be examined to see if they suggest strategic insights. Quite often, the best approach is to try several ways of empirically dividing the network in order to understand different aspects of the divisions within the network.

Cluster Analysis Based Interview Responses

Cluster analysis is another empirical data-exploration technique that groups together items based on their similarities or dissimilarities on a set of variables. Many statistical software packages, including network analysis packages, contain cluster analysis options.[7]

A very useful type of data that can be used as a basis for clustering stakeholders is the profile of mentions of global or intermediate categories of issues. It might identify, for example, a subgroup that is mainly interested in the environment or that focuses on issues of communications quality. More interestingly, it might group together those with concerns that appear unrelated at first glance. For example, it might cluster those who favor economic growth together with those who are most concerned about improving health care. This would suggest that these stakeholders think similarly at some level of generality. That insight would lead to further questions related to the strategic advantage of either strengthening or weakening the association between the economy and health.

Questions for Managers

These questions may help you decide what way the data should be summarized:

- What is the most frequently mentioned global category of issues? Which intermediate categories contributed the most to that high frequency? Which detailed categories contributed the most to the meaning of the intermediate category?
- Which intermediate categories are mentioned together the most in the interviews? Is this a result of the two categories meaning more or less the same thing, or is this connection more related to their cooccurrence in the real world? Is there an implied causal or consequential link between them?
- When thinking about how to calibrate the SLO scale, ask yourself what it would look like if your organization lost its SLO. Which resources would it lose access to? Are there threats of partial SLO loss as manifested in increased costs to access particular resources?

- Have several interviewees nominated another stakeholder that was not on the original list of interviewees? If so, ask yourself what assumptions led to that stakeholder being overlooked? What information can you get to test the validity of the assumptions?
- Are there any stakeholders who have indicated they have many relationships but who were not mentioned by those other stakeholders as relationship partners? If so, who can you talk to in the stakeholder network to validate that stakeholder's claim to being highly central in the network?

CHAPTER 6

Developing Strategies for Specific Issues and Their Stakeholders

By this point in the research process, you will have summarized the data from interviews with stakeholders. In this chapter, we look at ways to combine what you have in order to extract issues management strategies.

The ability to develop strategies improves with practice. However, an excellent way to increase your chances of getting the most out of your research the very first time is to immerse yourself in contextual information. Visit the geographic location of the controversy or the websites and blogs if it happens to occur in cyberspace. Studying the history of the controversy is always recommended. Many times a controversy is a mutation of a previous problem or dispute that was never successfully resolved. In addition, understanding the culture or subculture of stakeholders is invaluable. One seldom has the luxury of doing original anthropological studies, but often there are sociological or anthropological publications that can provide insights. It also pays to ask around to find local people who can articulately compare the local situation with situations elsewhere. This kind of contextual information makes the analysis of the interview information come alive and speak.

Extracting Strategies for Specific Stakeholders and Issues

This section deals with how to analyze the data for specific stakeholders and issues in order to extract strategies that apply to them. The subsequent section deals with how to extract strategies that apply to the whole stakeholder network. There are many overlaps between the individual-oriented techniques and the network-oriented techniques simply because the whole network is composed of specific stakeholders and their issues. Moreover, specific stakeholders and their issues are influenced, changed, and either included or excluded by dynamics afoot in the whole stakeholder network. The network affects the individual stakeholders and the individual stakeholders affect the network. Therefore, although we discuss these analytic techniques in separate sections, in practice your thinking must continually move back and forth between the individual stakeholder level and the network level.

Profiling Stakeholders

One of the most basic analytic techniques is to simply gather all the summarized data about a specific stakeholder and use them to construct a stakeholder profile. Usually it is not worth the resources to do this for every stakeholder on which you have data. There are two main ways to prioritize the stakeholders deserving of profiling. Sometimes you will want to do both, but often you can tell from a few preliminary comparisons if one or the other is going to yield the bulk of the insights.

Prioritizing Stakeholders for Profiling

The first prioritization method is to look at the centralities of the stakeholders. Those with highest eigenvector and betweenness centralities should be given top priority for profiling. The second prioritization method is to move to the level of clusters of stakeholders. The section of chapter 5 titled "How to Identify Separate Groups, Cliques, and Clusters" describes how to cluster stakeholders. If you find that your clusters are relatively homogeneous with respect to their opinions and well bonded with one another in the network, then you can average all their data and profile the clusters instead of individual stakeholders. Because there are usually only a handful of clusters, there is no need to prioritize among the clusters. Profile them all.

In the following discussion, we will assume that an individual stakeholder group is being profiled. To adapt the approach for clusters of stakeholders, simply replace individual-level data with means and per capita frequencies as appropriate.

Contextual Data

Stakeholder profiles amount to a presentation and qualitative synthesis of all types of data relevant to a particular stakeholder. This includes any historical or contextual information about the stakeholders. For example, such information might include the following:

- The purpose and main activity of the group
- The history of the group's involvement with the issue
- The geographic range of the group's membership or mandate
- Recent changes in the organization or group (e.g., leadership or mergers)
- Formal links with other groups (e.g., departments of government ministries)

Profile of Involvement With Issues

The analysis of frequencies of mentions of issues at the intermediate and global levels will have produced a row of mention frequencies for each stakeholder. These can be copied and pasted with labels for ranking from most frequent to least frequent. However, there will be some stakeholders whose mention frequencies are average. In order to distinguish these from others who are true champions of a particular issue, you can do tertile splits on the mention frequencies for each issue. A tertile split is nothing more than a division of all the stakeholders into three equal groups based on a variable. In this case, the variable is how often they mentioned an issue. The one-third who mentioned the issue more often than the remaining two-thirds can be given a tertile split label of 3. The one-third who mentioned the issue less than the other two-thirds would be given a label of 1. Those in the middle could be given a 2. Then it becomes easy to profile a specific stakeholder's involvement with issues. It is simply a matter of reporting all the issues for which they had a 3 in the tertile split data.

Sometimes scores of 1 have special significance as well. For example, if an environmental group had a 1 for mentions of an environmental issues, that would be noteworthy. It would be reason to examine the relationships between that group and other stakeholders who were in the top (3) tertile for mentioning that environmental issue.

Questions That Measure the Bilateral Relationship With the Focal Organization

The questions that measure the stakeholder's bilateral relationship with the organization at the center of the issues or controversy can be presented in individual bar graphs in order to highlight the finer details of the stakeholder group's attitudes. The graphs should show the mean for the stakeholder being profiled compared with the mean for all stakeholders.

If the bilateral section of the interview included measures of social capital, then Nahapiet and Ghoshal's cognitive and relational dimensions can be shown together with the means for the whole sample on the same measures.

Balance of Weak and Strong Ties

Turning to the multilateral data, it is worthwhile to examine the stakeholder's balance of weak and strong ties. Weak ties are relationships that were rated to have lower levels of social capital. Strong ties are relationships attributed with higher social capital (i.e., relationship satisfaction and shared goals).

Weak ties are adequate for exchanging information. It is a benefit to have weak ties in diverse parts of the stakeholder network for several reasons. The information flow allows one to find sought-after resources residing on other parts of the network more remote from one's closest friends. It also allows one to remain abreast of what is going on in the sociopolitical environment. This helps protect one's interests in terms of anticipating and responding to initiatives and alliances in other parts of the network.

Strong ties are needed to create sociopolitical alliances and to carry out collaborative initiatives. They not only involve exchange of information but also have the trust and shared understanding necessary to support exchanges of resources and the complementary joining of resources. However, because of the shared understanding, they tend to cause the parties to these relationships to discount novel outside ideas that could lead to innovation.[1] Therefore, a balance of weak and strong ties is usually a healthy sign in an organization. Stakeholders with a good balance of weak and strong ties are more likely to be able to achieve their objectives in the stakeholder network.

Who Is the Stakeholder Connected To?

In social network analysis, an "egonet" is the network of direct contacts of a single specified social actor. In profiling a stakeholder, the egonet often provides strategic insights. Social network graphing software packages usually provide a menu option for displaying each actor's egonet.

If you have selected stakeholders for profiling based on their eigenvector and betweenness centralities, then this part of the profile will show you quite a large number of connections. You can make the color of the stakeholder circles reflect the level of support for the project or the level of involvement in a particular issue. This will show you whether the stakeholder is connected with like-minded others or is maintaining a portfolio of contacts with diverse opinions. Each has different strategic implications.

If a high–eigenvector centrality stakeholder has strong opinions on an issue but is surrounded by others with more neutral opinions, there is a high probability that the stakeholder will influence the others to adopt more extreme opinions like his or her own. I once encountered a case where a highly central stakeholder (eigenvector centrality) with positive attitudes toward the focal organization in a controversy was surrounded by stakeholders with mildly positive or neutral attitudes toward the focal organization. Then an event occurred that turned that stakeholder's attitude extremely negative. Within a few months, the rest of the stakeholder's egonet had also moved toward the negative side. Highly central stakeholders can be true opinion leaders.

In another case, a stakeholder with high betweenness centrality had a positive attitude toward the focal organization in a controversy. The high betweenness centrality reflected the stakeholder's position as a bridge between business groups and environmental groups. The latter had quite negative attitudes. On its own accord, without any encouragement from the focal organization, the stakeholder began acting as a voice for moderation among the environmentalists. It organized a multistakeholder forum to discuss options and disseminate information. We did not have the opportunity to collect more data on how effective this was in moderating opinions, but the strategic implication is obvious. The well-positioned stakeholders can be powerful allies. Focal organizations need to identify them and engage them in discussions about ways to move the network toward productive dialogue and away from destructive rhetoric and polarization.

Profiling Issues

Issues can be profiled in much the same way as stakeholders. The section of chapter 5 titled "Issue Networks Based on Comentions" explains how to summarize responses to open-ended questions in a way that identifies the most mentioned issues or issue clusters. The section titled "Issue Networks Based on Attributed Consequences" shows how to identify the pivotal issues that offer the greatest potential for reframing controversies.

As with stakeholders, a qualitative description of the issue is very valuable. This would include its content features, its consequences, its history, and its implications for other issues.

These top-priority issues can be profiled in terms of which stakeholders or stakeholder clusters support or oppose them as they are currently framed. One technique is to list the top three stakeholders involved in a given issue and then look at their egonets simultaneously. Do their egonets overlap, or are they living in three separate social spheres? If they overlap, it is then informative to pare down the network graph to only those stakeholders that have relationships with at least two of the original three. If this is still a dense network, the criterion can be raised to having relationships with all three of the originals. If the network is too sparse, the number of stakeholder contributing their egonets to the network can be raised from three to four. Experimenting with different combinations like this gives you an indication of how organized the proponents of an issue are among themselves. Do they form a dense cluster with high bonding social capital? Are they spread throughout the network without much interaction among themselves? If so, is there a central player who could potentially introduce them to one another? If so, what is the attitude of that player? Depending on the nature of the issue, the focal organization may want to encourage or discourage such introductions.

When profiling issues, an important consideration is the extent to which the solution to the issue is potentially under the control of the focal organization versus uncontrollable by any one organization. Some issues can only be solved by cooperative action among many responsible parties. Figure 6.1 illustrates these two classes of issues, as well as how issues networks are connected to stakeholder networks. The lower portion of the graph is the network of stakeholders. The MGR is the person trying to the manage the issue for the focal organization. The upper part of the graph is the consequence hierarchy network of issues. The top and bottom layers are connected with dotted lines indicating which stakeholders are primarily concerned about which kinds of issues. The issues inside the oval on the top left deal with the activities of the focal organization. They are issues that the focal organization has the power to affect independently. The issues inside the larger oval on the top right are issues that no one organization can resolve independently. Their resolution requires many stakeholders to accept responsibility and to collaborate toward a solution.

The stakeholder network on the bottom has two clusters joined by a bridging stakeholder. The manager is presumed to be embedded in

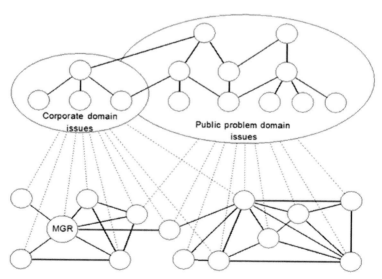

Figure 6.1. Conceptual illustration of how issue networks mesh with stakeholder networks.

the cluster of stakeholders concerned about things the focal organization can control. Yet some of those issues are also part of a larger public problem domain. This is where the manager may encounter the greatest difficulty. The focal organization may be blamed for things it cannot control. However, if the manager were to integrate the two clusters of stakeholders, then together with other responsible stakeholders, the issue could be addressed. Meanwhile the troublesome corporate issue would have been reframed as a public domain issue for which everyone shares some responsibility.

Bubble Graphs: Which Clusters of Stakeholders Have Which Clusters of Issues?

In chapter 5, we saw how a two-mode graph of issues and stakeholders could reveal which stakeholders were most concerned about which issues (Figure 5.1). The limitation of that way of representing the data was that they became too visually complex if anything more than the very strongest ties were shown. A more detailed representation can be achieved using bubble graphs. Most spreadsheets offer bubble graphs as a graphing option.

Bubble graphs allow us to directly compare the interests and issues of different clusters of stakeholders, improving our understanding of the similarities and differences among both the issues and the clusters. The graphs can be adjusted to show any level of mentions of issues by stakeholders. All mentions can be shown, or with a simple filter built into a spreadsheet, only the strongest can be shown. It is much easier to manipulate than a two-mode graph and much more interpretable when the number of stakeholders or issues is higher.

Figure 6.2 is a bubble graph that shows the clusters of stakeholders on the horizontal axis and the issues on the vertical axis. There are four clusters of stakeholder groups (A, B, C, and D) arrayed along the horizontal axis and five issues on the vertical axis.

In the body of the graph, the size of the circles (bubbles) reflects the per capita (per person) mentions of each issue per group. The larger the bubble, the more times the issue has been mentioned by that group, which indicates that this is a priority issue for this particular group. In Figure 6.2, all issues with a per capita mention of less than 0.1 have been suppressed. This increases the visual interpretability of the graph without losing interesting details.

The per capita number of mentions for issue 1 by cluster A was 0.85. This means that the thirteen members of cluster A mentioned issue 1 eleven times. If issue 1 were at the intermediate or global level, then it is possible that some members of cluster A mentioned issue 1 more than once. For example, one member might have mentioned it six times and another member five times, for the total of eleven. The per capita rate indicates mentions divided by the number of members of the cluster. It does not assume that every member of the cluster contributed equally to the total number of members. The per capita numbers in some of the bubbles are greater than one. This means that the issue was mentioned by that cluster more times than the number of groups in the cluster.

In Figure 6.2, clusters A and B have very similar concerns. Strategically this suggests two things. First, they are natural allies. If the network graphs show few connections among them, then it would be quite easy to encourage the development of relationships. In a case I studied in a developed country, the companies in the industry, who were defined as a cluster, had very few contacts with the business organizations in the surrounding towns, who were defined as another cluster. However, their mentions of the intermediate issues were nearly identical. We therefore

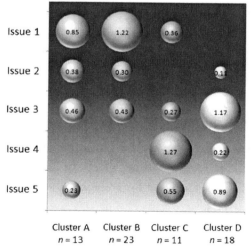

Figure 6.2. Example of a bubble graph.

recommended that the industry form alliances with the local business organizations in order to strengthen their legitimacy and extend their collective influence in the stakeholder network.

Cluster C in Figure 6.2 is preoccupied by issue 4. If the criterion for displaying bubbles were raised to 0.60, for example, there would be only one bubble in cluster C's column (i.e., at issue 4). The same would be true for clusters A and B (i.e., at issue 1). Cluster D, however, would stand out as a two-issue cluster. They were quite concerned about both issues 3 and 5.

Examining the rows of Figure 6.2, issue 3 is the only one that was mentioned more than 0.1 times per capita by all stakeholder clusters. Cluster D was most concerned about this issue, but cluster D could easily rally support for their concerns from all the other clusters. This raises the importance of issue 3 from a one-cluster issue to an issue with the potential for broad-based concern.

Issue 4, by contrast, was a true one-cluster issue. Only cluster C is very concerned about it. However, within cluster C, it is very important. If cluster C itself is composed of centrally positioned stakeholders who control critical resources, then issue 4 would have correspondingly high importance. By contrast, if cluster C were composed mostly of bystanders in the stakeholder network, issue 4 would be ranked as intermediate in importance.

Issue 1 is very important simply because it was mentioned so often by the two clusters that together contain more than half the stakeholders in the network. An examination of the profiles of those clusters may raise or lower that ranking.

Combining Analysis for Better Prioritization

Even more strategic insights can be gained by combining the bubble graph information with the network graphs of issues and stakeholders. For example, imagine that issue 1 corresponded to traffic on Figure 5.2 and issue 3 corresponded to dust. The high eigenvector centrality of these two issues and the linkage between them would suddenly create a basis for prioritizing the bubbles in the bubble graph. Obviously, issues 2, 4, and 5 would fade into the background. The implication would be that strategic initiatives should focus on issues 1 and 3 and on clusters A, B, and D.

Suppose further that in Figure 5.5, cluster D corresponded to the stakeholders with highest eigenvector centrality (i.e., B, D, and F) and that cluster A corresponded to the stakeholders in the bottom right (H, I, J, and K) who are connected to the rest of the network through the high betweenness centrality of one member (i.e., I). If these very influential clusters (as evidenced by their network position) joined forces to campaign on these very central and linked issues (as evidenced by the comention analysis), then there would be no question that an issue manager should focus efforts on issues 1 and 3 as viewed by clusters A and D. Devising initiatives would then require delving into the detailed levels of comments made by these stakeholders on these issues and combining that with contextual (e.g., historical, sociological, and political) knowledge.

Every controversy is different in some ways and the same in others. The analysis outlined previously focuses on regularities among controversies in order to set priorities. Once the priorities have been set, detailed action plans must be devised. That is when the things that make each controversy different start to matter more.

Scatterplots for Prioritizing Relationships

Some very strategic insights can be extracted from comparisons of stakeholders' scores on various variables. Scatterplots display the scores on two variables simultaneously for a set of stakeholders or clusters. They provide a visual way to quickly identify stakeholders who are prime candidates for special treatment. For example, stakeholders who are important to the focal organization but who report a poorer than average relationship with the organization would become candidates for relationship improvement.

Stakeholder's attitudes toward the focal organization can be gauged by responses to various bilateral relationship questions. Recall that if the controversy involves a focal organization, then the Stakeholder 360 interview includes a bilateral section. This section of the interview typically yields scores on a number of strategically important aspects of the relationship between the interviewed stakeholder and the focal organization (e.g., social capital in the relationship, motivation to collaborate with the focal organization, and level of social license to operate [SLO] granted).

In the following example, we presume that the level of SLO granted by each stakeholder has been measured.

Figure 6.3 shows the level of SLO granted by 26 stakeholders (i.e., A to Z) on the horizontal axis. This can be measured in the bilateral section of the interview using agree–disagree statements on a 5-point scale.

The vertical axis shows the stakeholders' level of influence in the network as measured by eigenvector centrality. The eigenvector centrality scores were produced by social network software and then transformed onto a 5-point scale in order to facilitate comparisons. Betweenness centrality is another measure of influence that could be used. Eigenvector centrality and betweenness centrality should be examined separately because they each offer different insights and cannot be merged without losing those insights.

In the example shown in Figure 6.3, most of the stakeholders fell toward the lower end of the influence scale because, in this case, only a few were very influential. This is not always the case. In networks where stakeholders operate collaboratively and collegially, they all tend to share the same level of higher eigenvector centrality with a few peripheral members falling to the bottom. This type of pattern occurs when the

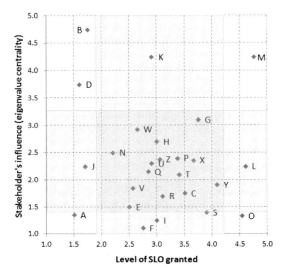

Figure 6.3. Scatterplot of stakeholder influence (eigenvector centrality) with the level of SLO granted by the stakeholder.

stakeholders have a great deal of bonding social capital and the mutuality that goes with it.

The rectangles inside the matrix of Figure 6.3 represent the 95% confidence limits around the means for influence and SLO. Stakeholders falling inside a rectangle are very probably (i.e., 19 times out of 20) average on that variable. The two rectangles divide the graph's matrix into four areas that are outside the average range on both measures (i.e., top left, top right, bottom left, and bottom right). In this case, the rectangles are quite wide because there were only 26 stakeholders. Figure 6.4 shows rectangles based on 81 stakeholders with the points in the graph representing clusters of stakeholders.

The top-right quadrant is where we find the stakeholders who are very influential but who granted a low SLO (i.e., B and D). These stakeholders require special attention. They should be profiled (see the section of chapter 5 titled "Profiling Stakeholders") in order to decide if their low SLO can be raised or their high influence can be lowered. Raising the SLO can be accomplished in a number of ways, all of which can be used simultaneously. One of the most effective is to change the impacts that the controversial activity has (e.g., reducing the carbon emissions, the noise, or the externalities in general). Another is to reframe that stakeholder's issues to emphasize different consequences or values. Another is to help them establish relationships with stakeholders who grant a higher SLO.

Lowering the influence of a stakeholder is more difficult. Over a longer period, the stakeholder's influence can be modified by attracting their potential allies or followers (i.e., influences) into clusters that grant a higher SLO. This can be done by using a combination of impact reduction, reframing, and relationship building (i.e., the three Rs).

In the bottom-left corner of Figure 6.3, stakeholder A stands alone as the only one who is low in influence and who has withheld the SLO. My experience has shown this quadrant to occasionally contain stakeholders who either are so uninvolved with the issues that they border on not even being stakeholders or who are so extreme in their opinions that they are shunned even by other opponents of the focal organization's activities. However, one must exercise caution in interpreting any graph that uses centrality data. Centrality scores are strongly affected by whether or not the stakeholder was actually interviewed or, alternatively, was only rated by others who nominated the group as being both a stakeholder and an important relationship for them. The latter will have low centrality simply because they have not been interviewed and therefore have not reported all their connections.

The top-right corner of Figure 6.3 contains stakeholder M. This stakeholder is influential and grants a high level of SLO. Strategically it would be advisable to foster relationships between this stakeholder and others who are low or moderate in the level of SLO they grant. If stakeholder M already has ample relationships like that, then the strategic priority should be to create initiatives in which M can explain the reasons for granting a high SLO.

The bottom-right corner of Figure 6.3 is populated by stakeholder O. This stakeholder grants a high SLO but has little influence in the network. A priority in this relationship would be to increase this stakeholder's influence. This would increase the general legitimacy and effectiveness of normative attitudes in favor of the focal organization's activities. The best initiatives for raising stakeholder O's influence would be those based on the stakeholder's existing concerns as expressed in the open-ended questions of the interview.

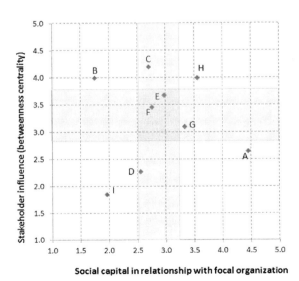

Figure 6.4. Scatterplot of stakeholder clusters' scores on betweenness centrality and social capital in the bilateral relationship.

Figure 6.4 shows the same general type of analysis with two different variables. In Figure 6.4, the vertical axis represents influence as measured by betweenness centrality. Those high in the graph tend to occupy more bridging positions in the network and therefore are more capable than others of controlling the flow of information and resources. The horizontal axis in Figure 6.4 is social capital with the focal organization. Those more to the right of the graph have relationships with the focal organization that would easily support close collaboration. The points in Figure 6.4 represent clusters of stakeholders. The position of each point is determined by the mean score of the cluster members on the vertical and horizontal variables. The graph summarizes data for 81 stakeholders. Each point has between 7 and 10 members. Because of the greater number of stakeholders, the rectangles are narrower than in Figure 6.3. The greater number of stakeholders increases the precision of the 95% confidence estimation of the mean.

The top-left corner of Figure 6.4 contains a stakeholder cluster (B) with high betweenness centrality but low social capital with the focal organization. The profiles of the stakeholders in this area should be examined closely to understand why the social capital is low. It could simply be that the stakeholder cluster is not very concerned with the focal organization's activities at the moment and therefore has little reason to develop a relationship. This would indicate that the cluster's stake is either small or dormant. However, if the profile indicates that the stakeholder is actively avoiding good relations, or even actively fomenting bad relations, then a relationship-level strategy is needed. The options generally involve reducing the stakeholder's influence or improving the relationship. They are not mutually exclusive.

Reducing cluster B's influence would involve creating other conduits for the flow of information and resources among different parts of the network. This has the advantage of creating more bonding social capital in the network and increasing its inclusiveness. If B had positioned itself as a bridge in order to accomplish the same ends, then B would see this as assistance and support. The result might even be that B's betweenness centrality slowly converts into eigenvector centrality. Working together with B in this way to make the network more inclusive would naturally provide opportunities for strengthening the relationship and increasing the social capital that B perceives in the relationship.

The other basic strategic option would be to focus on improving the relationship with B directly. If the examination of B's profile revealed that a specific issue was causing the poor relationship quality, that issue would form a natural basis for dialogue. The strategy then depends on whether there is a change in focal organization activities that might reduce the problem or a reframing that might reduce its perceived impact. In any case, creating opportunities for constructive dialogue would be an essential part of improving the relationship.

The other corners of Figure 6.4 would require similar choices between changing influence levels and improving the relationship. Stakeholder cluster I in the bottom-left corner needs both. Circumstances will suggest which is easier to achieve. Stakeholder cluster A in the bottom-right corner needs more influence. Is there a sparsely connected set of stakeholders that A could bridge or even turn into a cluster? Stakeholder cluster H in the upper-right corner only needs encouragement to use its influence.

The stakeholder clusters toward the middle of Figure 6.4 also provide strategic opportunities. The question is which of them could more easily be moved toward the upper-right corner. Again, answering the question depends on combining the view from this analysis with the insights provided by the other analyses described previously.

Network-Level Strategies: Applying Templates

The strategies discussed to this point have started with the characteristics of specific stakeholders. Then changes are planned that ultimately affect the structure of the network. An equally important approach is to start with the characteristics of the whole network. They suggest changes that ultimately affect relations with specific stakeholders. The former was a bottom-up approach. Now let us look at a top-down approach.

The section of chapter 3 titled "Implications of Templates for Governance and Issues Management" discusses the top-down strategies one would use if the stakeholder network resembled any of the nine templates of the bonding–core–periphery typology shown in Figure 3.3. Here we will elaborate on the more common templates with examples from actual cases. The more common network structures in my experience are those four in the upper right of Figure 3.3. They are shown in Figure 6.5.

In all these cases it is assumed that the accountable leadership network structure offers the best prospects for resolving issues in a way that is satisfactory for all. It is more likely to avoid problems like unjust reputation damage, long delays in issue resolution, and the illegitimate loss of resource access. In other words, it offers the best guarantee of a fair hearing and progress toward resolutions that benefit everyone.

Committee or Tribe

Figure 3.2 shows clusters on the bottom left and bottom right that have the structural characteristics of the committee/tribe template. The committee/tribe has plenty of bonding social capital but typically suffers from low economic performance (e.g., poverty) owing to a lack of bridging and linking social capital. The following case describes an African agricultural region that appeared to have an exclusive elite structure at first glance (i.e., bottom right of Figure 6.5) but upon closer inspection turned out to be more of like the committee/tribe structure (top left of Figure 6.5). Moreover, the happy outcome of the case was achieved through increasing the bridging and linking social capital in ways that moved the network structure more toward something resembling a wing in the accountable leadership structure.[2]

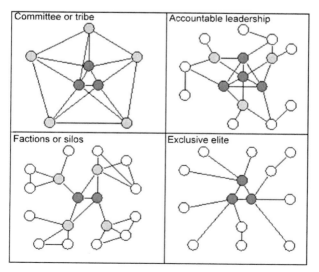

Figure 6.5. The most common network structures.

A multinational corporation (MNC) in the textile industry sought a secure supply of cotton for its mill in an African country. The MNC wanted to explore the possibility of lowering input costs by reactivating a cotton-producing area that had stopped producing for a number of historical socioeconomic reasons that no longer held sway over the region. The purchase of agricultural land by foreign corporations was politically unpopular. However, this MNC believed it could use the superior stakeholder relations it had already established in the country to secure a supply of cotton without buying the land. Indeed, with the help of their national government connections, they were able to lease a farm in one of the poorest states of the country. Using the farm as a demonstration project, the MNC showed that the land could produce the highest cotton yields in Africa for rain-irrigated cotton. However, to make the resource economical, they would need cotton from much more land. To get that, they would need to convince local farmers to begin training and start growing cotton. This would require the cooperation of state officials and local tribal chiefs. These local authorities were the real resource access gatekeepers. How could the company win an SLO from them?

At first, it looked like the chiefs and, to some extent, the government officials were each at the core of an absolute dictator structure (see bottom-right panel of Figure 3.3). They required regular gifts and personal favors, as one would expect from a dictator corrupted by power. However, a closer examination of the social safety net in African tribal society reveals that these leaders, especially the chiefs, were under close scrutiny by the members of their tribes. They had a responsibility to distribute their wealth throughout kinship and tribal networks as part of the traditional social security arrangements of the society. The chiefs, in fact, were continually worried about being seen as good providers. This suggests a network structure more like the committee/tribe of Figure 3.3 (top-center panel).

The MNC realized that to win the cooperation of the chiefs, they needed to (a) help the chiefs help the members of their tribes and (b) help the chiefs take credit for improvements in local conditions. The company built goodwill by instituting a mobile medical clinic to deliver health care to more remote villages in each chief's region. They further buttressed the goodwill by demonstrating the requisite respect for the chiefs required by protocol and by enhancing their prestige with demon-strative gifts and favors. Eventually the chiefs and elders went to the state officials from their tribes and expressed their support for the MNC's plan to expand production through a grower's program. Again, state officials needed help to provide for their networks of dependents. The lands that were owned by the state officials were therefore included in the grower's program. Once the program got started, farmers were making four times the income they had been earning previously by growing maize. The program was so successful for both the MNC and the farmers that neigh-boring states began inquiring about how to participate.

The case illustrates how understanding the cultural context helps in interpreting which template is the closest match. It also illustrates the power of combining bridging, bonding, and linking social capital (see Figure 3.2). The chiefs were leaders of bonded groups. The state offi-cials had the resources to create the bridges across the tribal and subtribal locales. The MNC had the linking social capital that connected the region to the global economy.

Factions or Silos

The town of Huarmey in the Peruvian Department of Ancash hosts a Pacific seaport for the export of copper from the Antamina mine. The mine is only 125 km east in a straight line but is also 4.5 km above sea level. Therefore, the pipeline that transports the copper slurry from the mine to the port covers a distance of over 300 km. Because Huarmey is near the mouth of two rivers, it has an agricultural base in an otherwise arid coastal region. There are several fishing communities nearby, and the Pan-American Highway provides some employment in services for truck-ers. The building of the port and its associated slurry dewatering plant in 2000 helped spur an influx of job seekers from poorer regions. During interviews in 2004, several stakeholders mentioned that the newcomers formed separate communities unto themselves and that the truckers had attracted prostitutes and drug dealers to the town.

The construction of the copper exporting port in Huarmey was con-troversial. Most of the issues revolved around environmental concerns. The water extracted from the slurry was not suitable for irrigating food crops. The company used it to irrigate a tree farm that was intended to provide local people with wood for construction. The pipeline itself was built at the urging of environmentalists who objected to the original plan of building a haul road through a forested area higher in the Andes. However, a different group of environmentalists were alarmed that the water from the slurry might somehow contaminate the ocean or the aquifers.

There were protest marches during the construction. An Antamina vice president was temporarily held hostage. Different groups brought forward different complaints, each without reference to the other. The company set up an environmental monitoring program to prove that it was not contaminating the environment. A group of fishers nonetheless demanded compensation for the pollution of their bay. They admitted that there had not yet been any pollution, but claimed that it was inevitable and that when it happened they would be entitled to compensation. They argued that if they were going to receive compensation someday anyway, why not now? Why should they have to wait? The media reported that fishers were demanding compensation for the company's pollution of the bay. The media did not report that the fishers admitted that no pollution had yet occurred.

While we were conducting interviews with stakeholders, a radio station interviewed an environmental leader who claimed that the monitoring had shown levels of heavy metals above the allowable limit and that the company had suppressed the results. The next week the station made a brief announcement correcting the environmentalist's claims. Indeed, over a year earlier a single weekly reading for a metal not found in the slurry did slightly exceed the tolerance limit. The reading returned to the acceptable normal range thereafter. The company did indeed postpone issuing warnings based on that one reading, preferring to confirm the problem with a subsequent reading before issuing an alarm. There was never another out-of-range reading. So what prompted the environmentalist to raise the alarm in a radio interview? Two stakeholders we interviewed offered an explanation. They claimed that a local environmental group had been infiltrated by members of the Tupac Amaru Revolutionary Movement, the Peruvian anticapitalist terrorist group that was in the process of disintegrating at the time of the interviews.

While the company was dealing with repeated false charges of environmental pollution, several community leaders in Huarmey were concerned about a different set of issues. The essence of their worries amounted to a lack of community cohesion. The town was unable to come together to form a consensus on priorities. Drug use was spreading to the town's young people. More new arrivals were adding to the unemployment problem. The farmers, the fishers, and the newcomers all wanted different things and never talked to each other.

The results of our stakeholder network analysis confirmed this view expressed by a few of the better connected community leaders. The general level of social capital was very low. Compared to other stakeholder networks, not many stakeholders had strong contacts with other stakeholders. Moreover, although there were a few scattered stakeholders with some centrality, these few were not strongly integrated into a clear network core. The left side of Figure 6.6 shows the strongest relationships in the Huarmey stakeholder network. The right side shows the closest template that it matches from Figure 6.5 (i.e., factions/silos).

The stakeholder labeled A on the left side of Figure 6.6 is the core. In this case, it was the municipality. The semiperiphery consists of additional influence centers with at least six strong ties each (i.e., B, C, D, and E). This pattern bears some resemblance to the accountable leadership structure (i.e., top left of Figure 6.5). However, the crucial difference is that stakeholders B and D are not directly connected to the core (A).

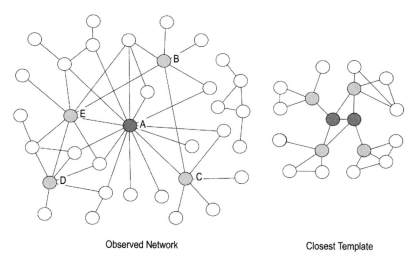

Observed Network   Closest Template

Figure 6.6. Huarmey's stakeholder network and the template it most resembles.

Moreover, there is a completely disconnected component in the network: the five-stakeholder cluster on the right-hand side consisting of a triangle with two pendants. It happened that they were mostly fishing groups. Therefore, the picture more closely resembles a weak core surrounded by separate power centers or factions.

The Huarmey stakeholder network illustrates the point that the templates in Figure 3.3 (of which Figure 6.5 is a subset) are only idealized icons. The degrees of closure structure and core–periphery structure are actually continuous. Therefore, there can be an infinite number of combinations of the two variables. These combinations occupy the theoretical spaces among the nine templates—the spaces where the lines of the matrix indicate boundaries. In reality, there are continua where the boundary lines appear.

It is quite possible that during the construction of the port, the Huarmey stakeholder network was more similar to the factions/silos template than at the time of the interviews. The interviews were done 3 years after the completion of construction. The network may have begun evolving toward a more accountable leadership structure. Certainly that was the aim of several key stakeholders (including the core). It was also our recommendation to the company to strengthen the core in order to more closely approximate an accountable leadership structure. The hope was that a stronger core could enforce norms of conflict resolution that would exclude hostage taking, false accusations, and spontaneous blockades prior to dialogue.

Exclusive Elites

San Marcos is at the other end of the pipeline from Huarmey. Although it is affected by the same company, its sociopolitical dynamics are completely different. In 2004, the town had a population of around 7,000. It is 3 km above sea level but 1.5 km lower in altitude than the mine site. The economy is mostly agricultural. Llamas and sheep graze on the hillsides. In the nearby valleys, there is some grain cultivation. San Marcos itself has a postsecondary training center partially supported by the mining company. In 2004, at the time of the stakeholder interviews, the Internet access provided by the company had spawned 13 Internet cafés that were packed with youths every evening.

The promising prospect for the town was the possibility of "Machu-Pichu-like" tourism through the development of the Chavín ruins. Outside San Marcos, the government was developing the tourism potential of an underground city built so that the corridors align with the Sun's rays on the summer and winter solstices. The ruins were judged to be more than a millennium older than Machu Pichu. A new highway was also under construction to make it easier for tour buses to reach the site.

San Marcos was the market and supply center for several surrounding villages and *comunidades campesinas*. A *comunidad campesina* is an administrative structure with authority over communal grazing and water rights, among other things. The politics of the region was dominated by two elite families that used to own most of the land. The mayors of San Marcos have always been members of, or aligned with, one family or the other. The issues that the mining company faced in San Marcos had more to do with prioritizing development projects (e.g., water infrastructure or a stadium). The issues in the *comunidades campesinas* around San Marcos included unresolved resentments about a resettlement that had taken place before construction and complaints about the effects of noise from blasting. While trying to resolve these issues, the company was also trying to help San Marcos without becoming enmeshed in the political competition between the current mayor and the former mayor.

The left side of Figure 6.7 shows the stakeholder network for San Marcos. The right side shows two absolute dictatorship (bottom right of Figure 3.3) templates linked together. The graphs are very similar. The two elite families are represented by the current mayor and the former mayor. They dominate the political landscape at the level of the relationships with the strongest social capital. At the level of relationships with a medium level of social capital, there were far more relationships between the two camps. These mostly involved organizations in the education sector. This observation led to the recommended strategy: In order to help San Marcos but also avoid getting caught in the us-versus-them dynamic, it was recommended that the company focus more on the education sector. This had the added benefit of raising the probability that the company could hire and contract locally.

The San Marcos example illustrates two things. First, local politics can turn well-intentioned efforts into community relations problems. If a company decides to support a development project advocated by one political party, it risks alienating the other political party and its supporters. The problem becomes more serious if the other party starts campaigning against the company and the politician it has allegedly co-opted. Second, the case illustrates the importance of considering weaker ties in addition to the strong ties. It was the more integrative network of medium strength ties that offered the opportunity to bridge the political polarization.

Evolution From One Template to Another

Because the stakeholder network approach to issues management is relatively new, we do not have many studies of how such networks evolve across time.[3] However, we do have some qualitative descriptions of stakeholder engagement processes that obviously must have included change in the structure of the stakeholder network over the years. In this section, we examine such a case and try to imagine how the stakeholder network was evolving from one template to another.

In 1972, a Canadian company known as Arctic Gas proposed to build a pipeline to transport natural gas from around the delta of the Mackenzie River on the Arctic Ocean. In 1973, a rival company, Foothills Pipeline,

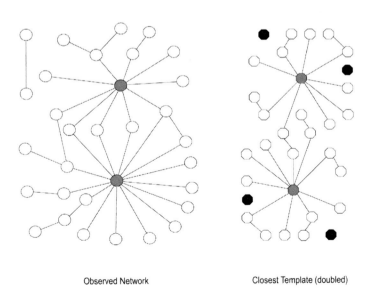

Observed Network   Closest Template (doubled)

Figure 6.7. San Marcos stakeholder network with the template it most resembles.

had launched a competing proposal for a smaller scale pipeline project. By 1974, the Canadian government had set up an inquiry to study
the proposals. In 1977, the inquiry concluded that the project should
be put on hold for 10 years in order to deal with aboriginal concerns.
Over the subsequent 32 years, the Déné people of northwestern Canada
negotiated their land treaties and their terms for allowing the pipeline to
go ahead. Then it was the Canadian government's turn to object to the
cost of its share of the deal. As of 2011, the project still has not yet been
approved.

The head of the first government inquiry, Peter Berger, began the consultation process with aboriginals by going to talk with them in their
meeting halls, in their homes, and out on the land in tents and in the
open air.[4] The consultations continued for nearly forty years. An entire
law specialty developed in Canada to deal with aboriginal affairs. Some
retired lawyers have spent their entire working lives on this consultation.
Some aboriginal leaders started as the fiercest opponents of the pipeline
and ended up 40 years later supporting it. To date the most valuable
result appears to have been the settlement of land treaties. Nonetheless,
the fact remains that the pipeline is still a pipedream. What went wrong?

Maybe nothing. Maybe it just takes that long for an entire people to
reshape its social network to make it suitable for coping with a completely
novel challenge from the forces of globalization. We can only guess at the
network structure among the aboriginal stakeholders. From reports, it
appears that the four main groups of Déné were not organized internally
for negotiations on megaprojects with international impacts. They had
no reason to be. They were busy living off the land.

Many of the Déné lived in small villages, exploiting the surrounding forests, lakes, and rivers for food and fuel. This suggests that their
network structure would have been similar to the "no organization"
pattern in Figure 3.3. When the need arose for a negotiating structure,
they turned to their existing internal structure that consisted of four
First Nations (i.e., the Inuvialuit, the Gwich'in, the Sahtuwill, and the
Deh Cho)[5] that would be affected by the pipeline. As these structures
developed the capacity to deal with the negotiations, the network structure probably came to look more like the separate clusters of Figure 3.3.
Slowly each of the four seems to have evolved into something like the
committee/tribe structure. Then in 2000, they joined together, forming

the Aboriginal Pipeline Group.[6] At that point they began to resemble an accountable leadership structure. However, it then slid toward the factions/silo structure when the Deh Cho withdrew from the process. That is where it stands as of this writing.

In 1974, pipeline executives were talking about a 4- to 8-year process before the gas started flowing.[7] They had no idea how social network structures affect infrastructure projects. They were living in a period when social network graphs were being produced by hand. Eigenvector centrality had not yet been invented. Indeed, the first book on stakeholder theory[8] had not yet been published. Today executives have the option of including the structure of their stakeholder network in the planning process. They can make a more realistic assessment of what challenges lay ahead. More importantly, they can develop strategies and launch initiatives to move the network toward an accountable leadership structure faster.

Questions for Managers

This chapter illustrates the kinds of strategic insights that can be gained from using various analytic tools to examine a stakeholder network graph. The following questions assume that you have performed such analyses one way or another. It might be through data collected in a Stakeholder 360 type of study or it might be through information collected through a combination of meetings with field representatives and a review of available documents and websites. In any case, here are some things to consider when trying to extract a strategy from summarized data about your stakeholder network:

- Which clusters of stakeholders share the same issues or concerns? Do they have relationships with each other as well?
- Which issues resonate with your supporters or allies? Are there neutral or ambivalent stakeholders, or clusters of stakeholders, who are also concerned about those issues?
- Do those who support your activities or your stance on an issue know each other? Do they talk to each other? Are they connected well enough to take joint action on the issue?

- Are there any pivotal issues that separate reasonable opponents from extremist opponents? How could a combination of the three Rs (i.e., impact reduction, reframing, and relationship building) change the pivotal issue, and the issue network within which it is embedded, to create more common ground between your organization and the reasonable opponents?
- Is the controversy characterized by unethical or illegal activities on the part of critics? Legal remedies aside, what clusters of stakeholders have the collective legitimacy to condemn such violations of social norms? What combination of the three Rs would be needed to induce them to do so?
- Is your organization being blamed for something it cannot control? If there is no authority that has responsibility for the issue, how could one be created ad hoc? Who are the parties that share responsibility? Can they be convened to organize a collective response to the issue?

CHAPTER 7

General Issues Management Strategies and Metastrategies

Issues Management: In Whose Interests?

Issues arise from conflicting interests. Therefore, it seems ingenuous to ask whose interests are being served by issues management. Issues are like political contests: Each party is trying to win. Therefore, issues are managed in the interests of whichever contestant the manager is affiliated with.

All the parties are trying to frame and reframe the issue simultaneously. Moreover, all the parties have access to the techniques described in this book. Everyone is also trying to change the shape of the network simultaneously. This neutralizes any advantage the techniques presented here might confer. As a result, we remain stuck in "politics as usual." All parties seek to use the latest and greatest issues management techniques to put their opponents off-balance and gain advantage for their own interests. Sometimes the jousting goes on for decades, as has been the case with several companies in the oil industry. Is there any way out of this cycle of conflict?

If one's interests are taken as ends and issues management is viewed as nothing more than a technical means to promoting those ends, then the cycle of conflict is self-perpetuating. Breaking out of the cycle requires questioning the unwritten rules of the game. In this sense, the question in the title of this section can be taken to be a query about the nature of the contest itself. Is it a winner-take-all contest? Will there be one winner and several losers? In other words, are we assuming that the interests of all parties are absolutely irreconcilable? Or is there another possibility? Can issues management serve the shared interests of all stakeholders?

Objections to Seeking Common Ground

The answer, of course, is that it is logically possible for issues management, like all management, to serve shared interests. Most people would also agree that it is desirable. The serious debate begins around questions about how practical it is as an operating principle.

Views about what is practically achievable range from seeking big benefits for the widest possible circle of stakeholders to just avoiding objectionable losses for the essential few stakeholders who have the most control over access to essential resources. The latter view tends to be particularly prevalent among internal stakeholders in the focal organization. Project proponents, for example, will cite deadlines and budgets to bolster their objections that pleasing everyone is impossible and that attempts to find common ground are a waste of time and money. Hence they argue that seeking less common ground in a shorter time frame is more practical. These are legitimate concerns. However, if they become the only concerns deemed legitimate inside the focal organization, sociopolitical risks rise dramatically. Proponents of seeking very limited common ground with stakeholders have to be prevented from defeating themselves. They get so focused on the internal logic of budget and deadline that they often fail to realize when they are working against their own interests.

A variant of the same kind of objection asserts that dialogue is unnecessary because it is obvious what the stakeholders need. This view is often used to fast-track philanthropic projects for stakeholders without any consultation. The result is that even when stakeholders indeed need what is given, their resentments are heightened by the lack of respect shown in how it was given. Of course, the resentment always finds another issue to which it attaches itself.

At the other end of the spectrum, there are utopian idealists who see any process that leaves some people wealthier than others as a neoliberal or, more recently, a "neostructuralist" ploy[1] to perpetuate the injustices of the past. One does not have to subscribe to the absolutist idealism of these critics in order to note the legitimacy of the injustices they cite. They make a valuable contribution with their keen sense of conflicting interests. However, although they say they want a more just social contract, they object to the kinds of voluntary accord-making processes required for arriving at a legitimate social contract. They object to approaches that urge dialogue, inclusiveness, and collaboration on the grounds that, no matter what the outcome, inequality will remain. Their insistence on a perfect world sabotages progress toward a better world.

On the periphery of the issues management field, there are critics who would rather resolve conflicts of interest with a legal action than through a search for common ground. Again, they can make a valuable contribution. They help define which tangents of the issue are already regulated and which are the ungoverned central matters. Unfortunately, some get so narrowly focused that they cannot see when unenforced rules, or unenforceable rules, become irrelevant to the issue. In the worst cases they imagine that shuffling legal papers will solve an issue where there is no entity with sovereign jurisdiction at all.

People who subscribe to any of these views tend to approach issues management as a winner-takes-all game. The most self-assured among them dismiss the search for win–win solutions as either a waste of time or a sneaky trick. Even those who oppose each other end up collaborating to keep the rules of the contest focused on an I-win-you-lose outcome. These unspoken assumptions about the nature of issues management keep the field focused on short-term tactics and keep too many practitioners lurching from crisis to crisis. In the next section we look at how a stakeholder approach is well suited for creating the conditions under which a collaborative approach to issue resolution can emerge.

Obstacles From Inside the Focal Organization

From the previously mentioned issues it can be seen that many of the obstacles come from inside the focal organization. Before we deal with general strategies for ending fruitless conflicts among external stakeholders, let us consider the internal stakeholders.

In 1999 the Minerals Council of Australia published a report on a survey of mining company employees on their attitudes toward safety.[2] The executives generally said it was one of the top three priorities in their set of responsibilities. Middle managers counted it among their top 10 most important responsibilities. Workers seldom thought it was one of their responsibilities. Today it is difficult to visit a mine run by a publically traded multinational without being forced to take an introductory safety course in which it is proclaimed that safety is everyone's responsibility. It has become an accepted part of the industry's culture. However, the cultural change took about 15 years of sustained effort.

In the field of the stakeholders and their issues, it is still 1999. The executives all claim stakeholder relations as a top priority. Many middle managers recognize its importance. However, the frontline workers who have direct contact with stakeholders seldom see themselves as having responsibility for managing the company's sociopolitical risk. In purchasing departments, for example, the professional culture encourages viewing supplier stakeholders as economic adversaries. In most industries, and with national governments, the idea of supporting community stakeholders through local purchasing is not business as usual. The potential for the work of issues managers to be reversed by line operations is high. What can be done?

In the long term, the goal must be to get the whole focal organization to accept that everyone has a responsibility for stakeholder relations and the management of stakeholders' issues. Fortunately, the same strategies that apply to managing stakeholder issues and networks can be used inside the focal organization.[3] Moreover, the nine templates from Figure 3.3 can apply to an internal organizational network just as they apply to a stakeholder network.

Just as fortunate, many focal organizations are starting to adopt some form of social or sustainability reporting (e.g., global reporting initiative, sustainability reports, and corporate social responsibility [CSR] reports). These are gradually moving toward quantifiable measures and year-to-year comparisons. Therefore, the adage "What gets measured gets done" gives hope that the things measured and reported in social reports will get done. Because so many of those things deal with issues raised by stakeholders, social reporting is likely a driver of organizational change. It is likely spreading responsibility for managing sociopolitical risk into more and more branches and layers of large organizations.

In the short term, we cannot wait for the focal organization's culture to change. Therefore, a more limited goal is worth pursuing. Studies of interactions between and among networks suggest the dictum "Bond before you bridge."[4] Bonding before you bridge implies that the focal organization should at least develop an initial view of an issue before attempting to create alliances with others. The initial view should not be a fixed action agenda or policy position. It should, however, articulate how the issue affects to organization's interests (e.g., its access to resources). All parts of the organization should have a chance to contribute to the conversation that produces this perspective. It is likely that the perspective will become elaborated and altered through interactions with stakeholders. However, the initial position at least prevents the organization from inadvertently sending dozens of conflicting messages to stakeholders. It also familiarizes internal stakeholders with the dimensions of the issue so that they are better prepared for the impacts that managing it may have on them later.

Stabilizing the Sociopolitical Environment

In chapter 2 we looked at two models of the life cycle of issues (see Figures 2.3 and 2.4). In both cases, the regulation or governance of the issue comes last. The invention and framing of the issue is a creative act. It starts a new conversation in the public, sociopolitical arena. Therefore, the focal organization framed as being the culprit cannot have a response plan already prepared. There is an irreducible unpredictability about issues. However, that does not mean that chaos has to erupt. Even in the absence of regulation or ad hoc governance, or where it is unclear who has jurisdiction, a stakeholder network approach can lend stability to the sociopolitical environment.

The main nongovernmental sources of sociopolitical order are social norms, accepted practices, customs, and a general stakeholder consensus. The two main ways to bring these into play correspond to the two types of networks depicted in Figure 6.1—namely, the network of stakeholders and the network of issues. The issues management strategies associated with the stakeholder network focus on how to move toward an accountable leadership pattern. The strategies associated with the issues network deal with developing an issues frame that encourages everyone to take responsibility for collaborating toward solutions to agreed-upon priorities and goals. These two foci for change are shown in the rows on Table 7.1. The columns of Table 7.1 correspond to two major approaches for inducing change. They, too, divide themselves between an emphasis on stakeholders versus and emphasis on issues. The left column represents techniques that attempt to reframe the issues across the whole stakeholder network at once. The right column represents techniques that take a more gradual approach and focus on modifying the shape of the stakeholder network by changing relationships among stakeholders.

Even through the all-at-once reframing techniques focus on changing the structure of the issues networks, they have strong effects on the shape of the stakeholder networks as well. Similarly, even though the focus of the continual structural-modification techniques is to alter the stakeholder network, these modifications depend heavily on either reinforcing existing common ground on issues or reframing pivotal issues to create more common ground. In the following sections we examine how each set of techniques can contribute to stabilizing the sociopolitical environment in which issues traverse their life cycles.

All-at-Once Reframing

In some social contexts it is possible to deal with the whole stakeholder network at once, rather than relationship by relationship. There are several group-process techniques that bring all the stakeholders into one room at the same time. They can be one-time events or a series of meetings. For example, it is not uncommon for towns and cities that have

Table 7.1. Classification of Change Foci and Methods for Stabilizing the Sociopolitical Environment

		How to induce change	
		All-at-once reframing	Continual structural modification
What to focus on changing	Stakeholder networks	Because these techniques bring all stakeholders into one room, they raise the general level of social capital in the network.	These techniques depend on data on the stakeholder network. The templates then diagnose which relationships need creation or strengthening.
	Issue networks	These techniques encourage stakeholders to collectively produce a reframing of the issues that they all endorse.	Data from the same interviews identify pivotal issues that can be reframed to expand the common ground for new or stronger stakeholder relationships.

suffered a severe economic decline to use these techniques to define priority goals for their future economic prosperity.[5] These techniques often serve to stabilize a stakeholder network, not only by creating a set of common goals among stakeholders (i.e., reframing the cognitive dimension of social capital), but also by forcing the stakeholders to interact person to person (i.e., the relational dimension of social capital). If the stakeholders have adopted fixed positions on issues, these techniques create fluidity in the issues network. They encourage people to move toward shared visions for their collective future.

One such technique is known as the "appreciative inquiry summit." This technique brings together stakeholders in a four-stage process that focuses on their strengths and the values they want to see manifested in their collective future. It has been used with organizations and communities to break out of cycles of conflict and to move forward collaboratively. Another process known as "future search" is based on similar assumptions. Various other refinements and innovations for large group processes are intended to promote collective learning, innovative breakthroughs on conflicts, and the development of shared visions.[6]

These techniques are not part of the stakeholder networks approach to issues management per se, but they are mentioned here because they can be borrowed to support the stakeholder network approach. The reader can consult the rich literature on such techniques for details on how to use them. Here it is appropriate to simply add a few observations about when these all-at-once reframing techniques are most helpful.

When stakeholders come together all at once, they will form relationships. It is difficult to predict which relationships will be formed. This is not a problem in situations where any new relationships would be an improvement. For example, with less organized stakeholder networks (e.g., the three bottom-left templates of Figure 3.3), this technique is a quick way to give the whole stakeholder network more social capital.

If stakeholders have already formed themselves into clusters, they will tend to keep to their own groups when brought together in one of these sessions. In order to encourage the formation of more bridging ties, it is necessary to deliberately arrange seating at tables and during any activities.

It should not be assumed that the all-at-once reframing techniques are a faster way to get the same results as continual structural modification techniques. The all-at-once techniques do not permit the same precision in reshaping either the stakeholder network or the issues network. Moreover, they are not necessarily faster. Experience shows that trying to coordinate the schedules of all stakeholders so they can be in the same room at the same time can take many months. For example, if a key set of stakeholders believes legal solutions will eventually give them everything they want, they have no motivation to make an effort to participate in voluntary solutions. Similarly, groups can use their participation as a bargaining tactic, threatening to boycott the forum unless they can set conditions on the agenda. Moreover, all-at-once techniques sometimes fail in the sense that no comprehensive reframing emerges that has everyone's support. So many factors can contribute to such failures that it is difficult to predict the level of risk of failure beforehand.

Continual Structural Modification

The continual structural modification approach is based on the simple truth that we are all continually modifying the networks in which we participate. The only choice is between modifying them consciously or unconsciously. To modify them in ways that create more common ground for collaboration, a conscious plan is preferable. Stakeholder 360–type interviews provide the raw data needed to make conscious decision about what to try to modify. The templates from Figure 3.3 provide a framework for interpreting the data and setting priorities.

Moving Toward Accountable Leadership

The best strategy for fostering sociopolitical norms in a stakeholder network is to work toward shaping it into an accountable leadership structure (top right of Figure 3.3). If the stakeholder network has a structure approximating the accountable leadership pattern, then a solid majority of network members accept the legitimacy of the norms. The core, with the help of the semiperiphery, is powerful enough to bring norm violators into compliance, but they are also accountable enough that the norms themselves reflect input and acceptance from the periphery.

When a network with this structure establishes norms for the resolution of issues and conflicts, the norms have more legitimacy than those established by the other structures shown in Figure 6.5. The norms established by an exclusive elite lack inclusive input and support. The norms established by a faction or silo structure are unenforceable. The norms established by committee or tribe are based on isolation-induced intolerance of diverse perspectives.

The accountable leadership structure is equally effective in establishing an inclusive yet action-oriented framing for issues. It avoids having the agenda hijacked by a vocal faction, as would be the case in the factions/silo structure. It avoids allowing powerful groups to frame the issue for their personal benefit as happens in the exclusive elite structure. It also prevents a closed, bonded group from framing the issue without considering essential new information or outside interests.

The causality also works from issues to structures. If a stakeholder network somehow has achieved a consensus on how to frame the issues, then the stakeholders already have high cognitive social capital among themselves. This accelerates the rate at which they can then form themselves into an accountable leadership structure.

Moving Away From Dysfunctional Patterns

The core in the committee or tribe pattern (top center of Figure 3.3) has the ability to enforce norms and enjoys popular support. The main problem is that the isolation and inward-looking nature of the network confines it to a narrow range of information and perspectives. It suffers from parochialism and an exaggerated tendency to frame issues in terms of us versus them (everyone outside the tribe). To reduce these defects, create bridging social capital between the committee or tribe and outside networks. Care must be taken to insure that bridging actors maintain legitimacy inside the committee or tribe. It is very easy for the committee or tribe to simply reject anyone whose thinking gets too innovative or too far from the internal orthodoxy.[7] Here is where reframing pivotal issues can open mental pathways for the bonded group to accept new perspectives and interests.

The core in the factions/silos pattern (middle row in Figure 3.3) needs the durable support of more than half the semiperiphery in order to be able to enforce any norms. The strategy for accomplishing this would be to foster greater centrality for the moderate stakeholders and those with more willingness to seek common ground with others. As you may have noticed, my opinion is that the global economy as an emergent focal organization faces this type of stakeholder network. It is under attack from all quarters—even from its biggest beneficiaries.[8] It has no strong leadership or core capable of enforcing inclusive, multilateral dispute-resolution mechanisms or norms. In these types of situations, reframing issues on the basis of a more widely shared common ground (e.g., the interests of human survival) can help strengthen the core.

The exclusive elite pattern (center of right column of Figure 3.3) shows that an elite minority can set the rules and norms by itself. A majority is not necessary. Here the problem is a lack of accountability. The development of a semiperiphery would solve that problem. Generally that can be done by fostering connections among the semiperiphery. Exclusive elites realize this and often discourage such activities. For example, Falun Gong is a spiritual exercise movement based on traditional Chinese philosophy. The Communist Party elite imprisoned many of its leaders in an attempt to eradicate the practice. They realized that it was fostering connections among otherwise-unconnected members of the nonelite. They saw this as a threat to stability. The lesson is that one must be careful when fostering a semiperiphery. The elite may respond with repression. A deep understanding of local conditions is needed to find feasible and safe initiatives. In terms of how changes to the issues network can help, there is usually a need for more transparency and freedom for debate in these situations. Any reframing that broadens the permissible range of discourse is helpful. This is why artists and religious leaders often find themselves at the leading edge of structural change in such circumstances. Without being explicitly political, they attempt to broaden the field of acceptable discourse.

Lesser organized stakeholder networks need both bridging and bonding social capital, especially arranged in a pattern that creates a core–periphery structure with an accountable leadership. At times political contests arise between stakeholders with less organized internal patterns of social capital versus those with an accountable leadership structure.[9] Such cases emphasize three points.

First, the ability to convince others that one's issues are legitimate and urgent depends on having social capital. There is an interdependence between the influence of stakeholders and the influence of the issues they espouse (as implied by the vertical ties in Figure 6.1). Second, a lack of organization is relative in the context of stakeholder power struggles. The group with more social capital and a structure closer to accountable leadership has the political advantage. Third, networks exist within networks. Although it is not that common to find entire stakeholder networks with low social capital like the three lower left templates in Figure 3.3, it is common to find such patterns in subsections of a whole stakeholder network. The templates of Figure 3.3 can be used to analyze different sections of a network in order to assess the relative political influence of different groups.

There are many benefits to stabilizing a stakeholder network by moving it toward accountable leadership. The stable, long-term alliances involved in maintaining the structure can produce less damaging issue life cycles, more sustained resource access, political support from the former critics, innovations in ways of conducting focal organization activities, and early warnings about emerging issues.

Toward a Global Social Contract

In chapter 2 it was argued that more and more issues are occurring in sociopolitical spaces where there is no government in charge, either because of weak sovereignty, or because of holes in the web of jurisdictions. Therefore, increasingly issues only come to the resolution stage of their life cycles if some form of effective network governance can be constructed. In this chapter it was argued that an accountable leadership structure offers the best governance of stakeholder networks and therefore the best hope for issue resolution. It can be added that to the extent that network governance evolves into institutionalized governance (i.e., government), the accountable leadership pattern optimizes the chances of subsequent democracy and legitimacy.

The work of issues managers can contribute to improving social governance. Civilization depends on the achievement of social cooperation on a large scale. Large segments of the population must accept the bargain presented by the social contract. However, the concept of the social contract can be applied at levels below the whole society. It evokes a mutually negotiated view of social order, even in specific industries or sectors. Resolving issues is part of the ongoing process of negotiating the social order—and therefore the social contract.[10]

If this is done in many local places, it starts to accumulate into a bottom-up global social contract. The United States prospered in the 1950s and 1960s when, according to some observers,[11] it came close to having a widely supported social contact, which has fallen apart in recent years. If the United States is moving from an accountable leadership structure to something closer to an exclusive elite structure,[12] then it cannot be relied on to export a successful social contract template in this round of globalization. Such top-down approaches, from the developed world to everyone else, do not have a good history of success. A just globalization will require at least the addition of bottom-up approaches. That would involve the negotiation of many diverse accommodations among stakeholders from all sectors (e.g., business, government, and civil society) on a case-by-case and issue-by-issue basis.

The bottom-up approach to negotiating a global social contract at least has the promise of being genuinely legitimate. There are many such microsocial contracts being negotiated today.[13] The future may see some of them applied on a broader scale and to issues of global range. Several experiments have already begun.[14] To the extent that issues managers can move their stakeholder networks toward accountable leadership structures, they contribute to resolving this challenge that now faces humanity.

Questions for Managers

This chapter deals with the longer term planning horizon and the larger picture of issues management. It emphasizes how the stakeholder networks approach can contribute to societal ends while solving practical issues management problems. In taking up that challenge, issues managers need to consider the following:

- Who inside the focal organization could block progress toward reframing the issue in your organization's communications? What are their concerns and interests, and to whom are they connected in the internal network?
- What line functions inside your organization deal with stakeholders who are influential in the network? Which ones

perform activities related to your top-priority issue? Do they understand how strategic these stakeholders and issues are? Do they understand the part they play in managing the issues?

- Are the stakeholders likely to come to a meeting where they would all be in the same room? What is the worst that could happen if an all-at-once approach were attempted?
- Are there sections of your stakeholder network that lack social capital? If so, is it because their stakes are minimal or because they face barriers to becoming better organized?
- What role does the lack of governance play in creating and perpetuating the issues your organization faces? Would a network form of governance help stabilize or resolve the problem?

Notes

Preface

1. See Miller and Ireland (2005) and Wehmeier (2006).

Chapter 1

1. See Stevenson (2004).

2. See Norman (1999, 2004).

3. See Harvey (n.d.).

4. The first theoretical treatment of the term "stakeholder" was Freeman's (1984) seminal book, *Strategic Management: A Stakeholder Approach.*

5. Post et al. (2002) proposed the following more restrictive definition of a stakeholder: "The stakeholders in a corporation are the individuals and constituencies that contribute, either voluntarily or involuntarily, to its wealth-creating capacity and activities, and that are therefore its potential beneficiaries and/or risk bearers" (p. 19).

6. Driscoll and Starik (2004) nominated the natural environment as a stakeholder. Haigh and Griffiths (2009) extended the idea arguing that focal organizations not only affect the natural environment but are also affected by it, most dramatically by climate change impacts. However, Phillips argues that only people can be stakeholders because being a stakeholder implies having the capacity to reciprocate within implicit social contracts (2003, pp. 140–141).

7. Orts and Strudler (2002) and Phillips and Reichart (2000) argue that postulating nonhuman stakeholders diffuses the meaning of stakeholders to the point where the theory becomes useless to managers.

8. Note that to designate an emergent organization as a focal organization does not imply that the emergent organization itself is a stakeholder in anything. Such organizations seldom have the capacity for reciprocity and therefore could not be considered stakeholders.

9. Trist (1983) used the term "problem domains" to refer to interorganizational fields that affect and are affected by many stakeholders. Wood and Gray (1991) brought stakeholder terminology into the description of problem domains.

10. Several authors have identified networks as a type of organization that forms and changes without anyone being in charge (Calton and Lad, 1995; Edelenbos and Klijn, 2007).

11. Freeman and Evan (1990) discussed informal social contracts negotiated multilaterally among all stakeholders, not simply bilaterally between management and stakeholders. Mitchell et al. (1997) note that such a multilateral contracting approach implies a network perspective on stakeholders.

12. Stormer (2003) argued that a corporate-centric view of stakeholders is a poor conceptual tool for bringing awareness to the multiple dimensions and actors involved in emergent networks where there are shared problems.

13. Applying a similar distinction to the problem of stakeholder management, Roloff (2008) distinguished between corporation-focused stakeholder management and issues-focused stakeholder management. Coming to similar conclusions from a governance perspective, Bertels and Vredenburg (2004) began by examining three cases of partnerships among the public, private, and nonprofit sectors. They found that formal governance systems of the various types examined were all inadequate. Instead, they proposed moving from an organization-based view of governance to a problem domain–based view (Gray, 1989; Trist, 1983).

14. For more on the commons dilemma, see Cardenas (2002), Hardin (1968), and Ostrom (1990). Ackoff (1999) coined the term "mess" to mean a shared problem that no one organization can solve alone.

15. See Orts and Strudler (2009) for more on the limits of stakeholder theory as a source of ethical proscriptions.

16. Friedman (1970) came to be seen as an opponent of stakeholder theory because he asserted, in the title of a *New York Times* magazine article, that "the social responsibility of business is to increase its profits."

17. Agle et al. (2008) note the historical contrasting of stakeholder and stockholder interest.

18. In his book, *Supercapitalism*, Reich (2007) elaborated on his view of the post–World War II period as a high point in the achievement of a just social contract in the United States.

19. Freeman first elaborated on the separation fallacy in his 1994 article in *Business Ethics Quarterly*. With colleagues (Freeman et al., 2010), he recently expanded on the fallacy and the confusion it causes.

20. For examples of these approaches to stakeholders and corporate social responsibility (CSR) see Calton and Payne (2003), Isaacs (1999), Senge (1990), Bowen et al. (2010), and Svendsen and Laberge (2005).

21. Habermas's earlier position can be found in his book, *The Theory of Communicative Action* (1984).

22. For a discussion of this admission, see Scherer et al. (2009).

23. Maak (2007) argues that the activities needed to win political battles often require increasing the social capital in networks and therefore have at least some prosocial effect on society, regardless of the content of the political issue.

24. Richter (2010) attempts to identify the liberal democratic assumptions in various threads of CSR thought.

25. See Phillips (2003).

26. Donaldson and Dunfee (1999) were the first proponents of integrative social contracts theory.

27. See Fassin (2009) for a refreshing exception.

28. "Not in my backyard" (NIMBY) is the refrain often heard from neighbourhood groups that oppose the location of a facility in their area even when the facility is necessary or beneficial to the community as a whole. For example, proposals for the location of municipal garbage dumps usually elicit NIMBY reactions from nearby residents or residents along the haul routes. Proposals for new highways or ports also frequently provoke NIMBY groups. The response even appears in reaction to proposals that would cause change that many (e.g., sustainable housing supporters, low-income people, or urban lifestyle enthusiasts) would consider improvements, such as the construction of higher density residential buildings in a zone currently containing only single-family houses.

Chapter 2

1. For a formal statement of "the resource view of competitive advantage," see Barney (1996). For a review that includes the subsequent broadening of the perspective, see Barney et al. (2001).

2. Bowen (2007) discusses the Vodafone case in which building a stakeholder network was the key to success. Litz (1996) and Russo and Fouts (1997) discuss the competitive advantages of gaining legitimacy in stakeholders' eyes—for example, on social and environmental issues.

3. See United Food and Commercial Workers International Union (2011a, 2011b).

4. For more details, see Bhattacharya (2008), Evans (2008), "Farmers Block Roads" (2008), and Srivastava (2008).

5. News reports are inconsistent regarding the number who died and the number of attackers.

6. There is an enormous amount of information available online about this case. Some of it is inconsistent or contradictory. Here are the sources I used to piece together the story: "Anti-Mining Demonstrators" (2007), Kennard (2010), "Monterrico Metals" (2005), "Monterrico Metals Company" (2011), "Peru Industry Revolt" (2007), "Rio Blanco Torture" (2009), "Three Workers Died" (2009), "Two Die in Attack" (2009), and "UPDATE 2" (2007).

7. The fullest published statement of the theory to date is in Thomson and Boutilier (2011). Shorter versions appeared in Boutilier and Thomson (2009).

8. Joyce and Thomson (2000) described the historical conditions in Latin America that make obtaining a social license so important there and offered some advice to extractive resource companies on how to get and keep it. Nelsen and Scoble (2006) did a study of perceptions of the meaning of the term in the mining industry.

9. Mahon and Waddock (1992) proposed an integrative systems model. Regester and Larkin (2008, p. 50) presented a model that is popular in the field of public relations. The model shown in Figure 2.3 is a modification of a model by Post et al. (2002) published in an earlier version of their textbook on business and society.

10. The concept of framing originally came from the school of sociological social psychology known as symbolic interactionism. Goffman (1974) popularized the term.

11. The study of social movements is a subfield in sociology. For more information, see Snow and Benford (1992), Diani (2003), and Gamson (1997).

12. These data are from the U.S. Energy Information Administration (2009).

13. See the report by Salazar (2009).

14. Internet sources on this case contain polarized views. Some are sympathetic toward the warriors ("Caledonia Land Claim," 2006), and some are sympathetic toward their victims (Blatchford, 2010). A few report events without taking sides (e.g., Nolan, 2010).

15. Although they use different labels and discuss these types of governance in different context, there is a remarkable consensus on the basic concepts (Goldsmith and Eggers, 2004; Jones et al., 1997; Powell, 1990).

16. Eddy and Baetz (2010).

17. Ouchi (1980) claims that clans are the default. Anthropologists have embraced social network analysis as a tool for describing the structure of such forms of organization. Clans are essentially networks.

18. The classic work on legitimacy in organizational and management science is Suchman's (1995) review article.

19. Richter (2010) asserts that current conceptions of corporate social responsibility (CSR) not only assume an often-unrealistic level of rule of law but also go too far in assuming a functioning democracy and a healthy nation-state. Lumping them together under the label of "liberal democracy assumptions," Richter argues that a new concept of CSR is needed. He suggests "stakeholder democracy" as a possible source of more universal legitimacy.

20. Waddell (2003) coined the term "global action networks" and has studied many examples of them (Waddell, 2007). Gray and Hay (1986) describe a national-level example of a legitimizing governance network, and Gray Gricar and Brown (1981) offer a local example.

21. Indeed, smoking rates have declined in the United States ("State Smoking Rates," 2010; Stringer, 2007).

22. The terms "modern" and "postmodern" are used here in the same sense as in the World Values Survey (Inglehart and Baker, 2000).

23. See Hawthorn (2011).

24. See Boutilier (2005) for a typology of views toward sustainability that uses the categories of traditional, modern, and postmaterialist or postmodern.

25. The classic statement of this distinction was by Petty and Cacioppo (1986).

Chapter 3

1. Readers interested in reviews of the debate should read Adler and Kwon (2002), Glanville and Bienenstock (2009), Nahapiet and Ghoshal (1998) and Portes (1998, 2000).

2. Nahapiet and Ghoshal's (1998) cognitive dimension was elaborated further by Tsai and Ghoshal (1998).

3. Adler and Kwon (2002), p. 23.

4. Perhaps the most comprehensive typology of capitals is Roseland's (2005) list of six types: natural, physical, economic, human, social, and cultural. He defines natural capital as the stock of assets from the natural environment (e.g., fertile soil, potable water, and minerals). Physical capital consists of the human-made material resources such as equipment, buildings, machinery, and other infrastructure. Economic capital consists of the institutionalized patterns a community or society has for allocating material resources (e.g., via markets) and making decisions about physical and natural capital. Following Becker (1964), Roseland defines human capital as the knowledge, skills, and personal attributes that facilitate the creation of personal, social and economic well-being. Roseland adopts the Organization for Economic Co-operation and Development's (OECD, 2001) definition of social capital as "the relationships, networks and norms that facilitate collective action" (p. 9). Roseland's definition of cultural capital is similar to Bourdieu's (1980) in its emphasis on shared customs, traditions, and values and heritage. However, Bourdieu specifically includes artifacts and educational degrees. This allows him to use the concept at the subsocietal level in order to distinguish the cultural capital held by different social classes within a society or by different professional groups within a society (Bourdieu, 1989). Loury (1977), for example, concluded that even with equal ability and education (i.e., human and cultural capital), Black Americans would have more difficultly advancing economically (economic capital) owing to a lack of social capital (e.g., network contacts) with people who had the kind of social capital (connections) that could facilitate career advancement.

5. Bickart et al. (2010) found that the size of people's social networks (i.e., the structural dimension of social capital) correlates with the volume of the amygdala, a part of the human brain. Moreover, the immediate effects of influence and solidarity have been observed in the networking behavior of Macaque monkeys ("For Macaques," 2010).

6. This approach was more popular in political science that other social sciences (Helliwell, 2006; Helliwell and Putnam, 1999; Putnam, 2000).

7. Gittell and Vidal (1998) are credited with coining these terms.

8. Woolcock and colleagues developed a theoretical description of linking (Szreter and Woolcock, 2004; Woolcock, 2002). See Krishna (2001), Molinas (2002), Narayan (1999), and Narayan and Cassidy (2001) for examples of empirical research showing the importance of bridging, bonding, and linking social capital.

9. Bhalla (2002) completely and mercilessly demolishes the notion that globalization is bad for the world's poor. He even describes how that implausible idea arose and then spread. Dollar (2005) and Sachs (2005) added a few extra nails in the coffin.

10. These are some of the most dynamic and exciting approaches in each subfield. For examples in organizational development, see Burt et al. (2000), Gargiulo and Benassi (2000), and Moran (2005). For examples in entrepreneurship, see Steier (2000). See Bouty (2000) and Phelps (2010) for examples in innovation. Illustrative applications in the theories of the firm have been provided by Nahapiet and Ghoshal (1998) and Oh et al. (2006). For exemplary applications related questions of inter-firm alliances, see Blyler and Coff (2003), Inkpen and Tsang (2005), and Knoke (2009).

11. See Boutilier (2007, 2009).

12. For the seminal work in the social sciences on social capital, see Bourdieu (1980) and Coleman (1988).

13. This governance function of networks has been illustrated in the research literature on multisectoral collaboration (Wood and Gray 1991, Waddell 2003), collective action dilemmas (Ostrom et al., 2003), and networks of local governments (Cepiku, 2008).

14. Bowles and Gintis (2002) discuss the us-versus-them dynamics that produce failures in network governance in community settings. Meuleman (2010) finds that the best success comes from using all three type of governance blended together through metagovernance principles that make the mix more compatible with the cultural preferences of the society in question.

15. Bridging fosters innovation (Bouty, 2000) and is associated with a higher probability of promotion among business managers in different countries (Burt et al., 2000). However, it has also been found to characterize terrorist networks (Krebs, 2002) and insurance fraud networks (Burt, 2001).

16. The term "structural hole" was developed by Ronald Burt. He described mathematical formula for calculating the degree of bridging a network actor enjoys (Burt, 2001).

17. Gould and Fernandez (1989) identified five different types of brokerage positions (i.e., liaison, mediator, itinerant broker, representative, gatekeeper, and coordinator) and described how to measure them in a network.

18. The core–periphery concept has been used for many decades to describe the structure of cities. Wallerstein (1979) applied the concept to the international economy. He argued that it had a structure consisting of a core of wealthy countries, a semiperiphery of emerging countries, and a periphery of poor countries.

19. Onyx and Bullen (2000).

20. Crystallex International (2011).

21. Ross (2001) assembled statistics showing that oil wealth is associated with a drift toward authoritarian government.

22. De Waal's book, *Chimpanzee Politics* (de Waal, 2000), shows how deeply ingrained politics is in our biology. Bonding social capital, for example, has been shown to pay political rewards among Macaque monkeys ("For Macaques," 2010).

23. Wheeler et al. (2002) describe Shell's struggle in Nigeria to have relations with community stakeholders match the corporate social responsibility (CSR) pronouncements from the corporate level.

24. Mouawad (2009).

25. Janis (1972).

26. Lomnitz and Pérez-Lizaur (1987) describe the general elitist attitude in their study of a Mexican elite family. Elite Mexican businesspeople view foreign businesspeople as gullible. They also view foreigners' attempts to impose international standards as an affront to their autocracy. The international experiences of Wilson and Wilson (2006, p. 159) confirm that Mexican elites are not much different from others in this regard.

27. Eno (2010).

28. Tuckman's (1965) theory of group formation stages has evolved into a more complex literature on team building.

29. Research by Hill and Dunbar (2003) confirmed estimates that the human brain might not be able to manage more than 150 direct network contacts.

30. Lincoln and Miller (1979) were among the first to juxtapose friendship networks with advice-seeking networks. Krackhardt (1990) showed that people who can more accurately perceive actual friendship and advice-seeking networks acquire more sociopolitical power.

Chapter 4

1. The late Russell Ackoff chose the evocative term "mess" (Ackoff, 1999) to describe these kinds of problems because they often put managers in the situation of being held accountable for outcomes they cannot control.

2. For guides on how to conduct a social impact assessment, see Barrow (2000) and Burdge (2003). The website of the International Association for Impact Assessment (http://www.iaia.org) references many more additional resources.

3. The origins of the term are murky. One of the earliest applications in the social sciences has been attributed to Coleman (1959). For the benefit of readers who are lucky enough to never have lived through a snowy winter, I will try to explain the analogy. When it is not too dry and powdery, snow can be picked up and compacted by hand into a ball. If such a snowball is rolled in the snow, the snow on the ground beneath it sticks to the ball. Thus the ball gets bigger with each revolution along the snow-covered ground.

4. Senge et al. (1994) have shown that the sequence of questions described here works in both developed and developing countries.

5. The original intent of the method was to discover effective brand image themes (Olson and Reynolds, 1983; Reynolds and Gutman, 1988).

6. Marketers were encouraged to use such findings to communicate with consumers at the level of consumers' values (Woodruff, 1997).

7. Brennan and Henneberg (2008) extended the notion of consumers' values to voters' values. Boutilier (2009) used laddering to uncover means–ends relationships among issues of concern to stakeholders.

8. Van Rekom and Wierenga (2007) suggest that few people really think in a hierarchical manner. They suggest that networks of consequential links among concept at all levels of specificity and generality would be flexible enough to yield a more accurate portrayal of natural thought structures.

9. The analysis was done in 2001 and the study was described in Boutilier (2009, p. 172).

10. For more information about the use of Stakeholder 360 techniques in Australia, see Australian Centre for Corporate Social Responsibility (n.d.).

Chapter 5

1. Delhey and Newton (2005) provide a list of trust levels for 60 countries.

2. For pictures of the monuments, search Google Images for "the Big Nickel."

3. International Network for Social Network Analysis (n.d.).

4. Different centrality measures yield different but complementary information. Friedkin (1991) argues that this gives them a theoretical unity.

5. Smith and Fink (2010) performed experiments to prove the effects of betweenness and eigenvector centrality on influence in networks. Figure 5.5 is based on their illustration of the difference between these two types of centrality.

6. Many are described by Hanneman and Riddle (2005), published in digital form at http://faculty.ucr.edu/~hanneman/nettext.

7. For technical description of cluster analysis methods, see Romesburg (2004).

Chapter 6

1. Rowley et al. (2000) illustrated this point with data from the steel industry and the semiconductor industry.

2. In their published description of this case, Sharma et al. (1994) did not use the terms "social capital," "bonding," or "linking" because they had not yet been invented. Nonetheless, the phenomena they described in the case illustrate these concepts very well.

3. For a study of how one stakeholder network evolved over a 4-year period, see Boutilier (2009, chapter 9).

4. See "Mackenzie Valley" (2011, January 11).

5. See "The Mackenzie Valley pipeline" (2007, March 12).

6. See Mackenzie Gas Project (n.d.).

7. See "The gas companies" (1976, June 5).

8. Freeman (1984).

Chapter 7

1. Murray and Overton (2011) explain the differences between neoliberalism and neostructuralism.

2. See SAFEmap (1999).

3. For an overview of the application to organizational structures, see Cross and Thomas (2009); Cross et al. (2009), and Johnson-Cramer et al. (2007).

4. Human and Provan (2000) studied the legitimacy-building efforts of two nascent industry networks. They noted two different sequencing strategies to address the need for recognition from both internal and external stakeholders. One of their networks chose to focus on internal stakeholders first (i.e., network members and potential members) and then communicate more with external stakeholders later. The other chose the opposite sequence. The network using the inside-out sequence survived and the other did not. In social capital terms, the inside-out sequence would be called bonding before bridging. The outside-in sequence would be called bridging before bonding.

5. See Partners in Salford (n.d.), The Strategy Board (n.d.), Collective Wisdom Initiative (n.d.), and Strutzenberger (2011).

6. For more details on appreciative inquiry, see Cooperrider and Whitney (2005) and Finegold et al. (2002). Weisbord and Janoff (1995) describe the future search process. Svendsen and Laberge (2005) outline principles for convening stakeholder networks and guiding them through a collective learning process that results in innovative solutions and a shared vision. Roberts (2000) describes elements of network approaches to large-group facilitation processes for dealing with issues that affect whole social systems, such as stakeholder networks, even when there is no agreement about what the problem is.

7. Westley and Vredenburg (1991) describe a case in which an environmental activist lost his organization's support because the tribe-like membership could not accept his innovative ideas.

8. More Germans reportedly are turning toward more negative views of international involvement and trade (Saunders, 2011). Similarly, in 2009, U.S. citizens were more in favor of isolationism than at any point in the previous 40 years (America in the World, 2009).

9. Brooks (2010) described bridging, bonding, and linking social capital among commercial fishers in South Australia. She did not use the templates of Figure 3.3, but she provided enough description to guess which templates came closest to the patterns she observed in various sections of the industry's stakeholder network. The core issue was that, in order to preserve fish stocks, regulators needed to balance the interests of commercial and recreational fishers. The regulators cut the number of commercial licenses by half. The recreational fishers had much more bonding social capital and were well linked to influential community groups, including the regulators. Brooks's description of the recreational fishers' network evoked the responsible leadership pattern. The commercial fishers were relatively more isolated, like the emergent broker in Figure 3.3. Brooks warned that the resulting comparative lack of social capital among the commercial fishers was a factor threatening the long-term survival of the commercial fishery. They were likely to lose future political contests with the recreational fishers over access to the remaining fishing grounds.

10. See Calton and Lad (1995) for an introduction to microcontracting between stakeholders and companies. Carrin (2006) believes that Rousseau's (1968) concept of the social contract has renewed relevance to today's organizational legitimacy challenges.

11. See Reich (2007).

12. Reich (2007) cites the declining middle class as a prime cause.

13. See Andolina et al. (2009) for examples.

14. See Waddell's (2003) documentation of global action networks.

References

Ackoff, R. L. (1999). *Ackoff's best: His classic writings on management*. New York, NY: Wiley.

Adler, P. S., & Kwon, S.-W. (2002). Social capital: Prospects for a new concept. *Academy of Management Review, 27*(1), 17–40.

Agle, B. R., Donaldson, T., Freeman, R. E., Jensen, M. C., Mitchell, R. K., & Wood, D. J. (2008). Dialogue: Toward superior stakeholder theory. *Business Ethics Quarterly, 18*(2), 153–190.

America in the World. (2009, December 4). More Americans seek "withdrawal from world" than at any time for forty years. Retrieved from http://america intheworld.typepad.com/home/isolationism

Andolina, R., Laurie, N., & Radcliffe, S. (2009). *Indigenous development in the Andes: Culture, power, and transnationalism*. Durham, NC: Duke University Press.

Anti-mining demonstrators blockade Peruvian roads. (2007, May 7). *Environment News Service*. Retrieved from http://www.ens-newswire.com

Australian Centre for Corporate Social Responsibility. (n.d.). Knowledge to succeed. Retrieved from http://www.accsr.com.au/html/stakeholderresearch.html

Barney, J. B. (1996). The resource-based theory of the firm. *Organization Science, 7*(5), 469.

Barney, J. B., Wright, M., & Ketchen, D. J., Jr. (2001). The resource-based view of the firm: Ten years after 1991. *Journal of Management, 27*(6), 625–641.

Barrow, C. J. (2000). *Social impact assessment: An introduction*. London, UK: Arnold.

Becker, G. (1964). *Human capital: A theoretical and empirical analysis with special reference to education*. Princeton, NJ: Princeton University Press.

Bertels, S., & Vredenburg, H. (2004). Broadening the notion of governance from the organisation to the domain. *Journal of Corporate Citizenship, 15*, 33–47.

Bhalla, S. (2002). *Imagine there is no country: Poverty, inequality, and growth in the era of globalization*. Washington, DC: Institute for International Economics.

Bhattacharya, P. (2008, September 9). Standoff over, Nano plant in West Bengal goes. *The Daily Star*. Retrieved from http://www.thedailystar.net

Bickart, K. C., Wright, C. I., Dautoff, R. J., Dickerson, B. C., & Feldman Barrett, L. (2010, December 26). Amygdala volume and social network size in humans. *Nature Neuroscience Advance Online Publication*, 1–2.

Blatchford, C. (2010, October 25). Caledonia: The town that law forgot. Retrieved from http://m.theglobeandmail.com

Blyler, M., & Coff, R. W. (2003). Dynamic capabilities, social capital, and rent appropriation: Ties that split pies. *Strategic Management Journal, 24*(7), 677.

Bourdieu, P. (1980). Le capital social. *Actes de la recherche en sciences sociales, 31,* 1–2.

Bourdieu, P. (1989). Social space and symbolic power. *Sociological Theory, 7*(1), 14–25.

Boutilier, R. G. (2005). Views of sustainable development: A typology of stakeholders' conflicting perspectives. In M. Starik, S. Sharma, C. P. Egri, & R. Bunch (Eds.), *New horizons in research on sustainable organizations: Emerging ideas, approaches, and tools for practitioners and researchers* (pp. 19–37). Sheffield, UK: Greenleaf.

Boutilier, R. G. (2007). Social capital in firm-stakeholder networks: A corporate role in community development. *Journal of Corporate Citizenship, 26,* 1–14.

Boutilier, R. G. (2009). *Stakeholder politics: Social capital, sustainable development, and the corporation.* Sheffield, UK: Greenleaf.

Boutilier, R. G., & Thomson, I. (2009). Establishing a social license to operate in mining [Online course]. Retrieved from http://www.edumine.com

Bouty, I. (2000). Interpersonal and interaction influences on informal resource exchanges between R&D researchers across organizational boundaries. *Academy of Management Journal, 43*(1), 50–65.

Bowen, F. (2007). Corporate social strategy: Competing views from two theories of the firm. *Journal of Business Ethics, 75*(1), 97–113.

Bowen, F., Newenham-Kahindi, A., & Herremans, I. (2010). When suits meet roots: The antecedents and consequences of community engagement strategy. *Journal of Business Ethics, 95*(2), 297–318.

Bowles, S., & Gintis, H. (2002). Social capital and community governance. *The Economic Journal, 112*(483), F419–F436.

Brennan, R., & Henneberg, S. C. (2008). Does political marketing need the concept of customer value? *Marketing Intelligence and Planning, 26*(6), 559–572.

Brooks, K. (2010). Sustainable development: Social outcomes of structural adjustments in a South Australian fishery. *Marine Policy, 34,* 671–678.

Burdge, R. J. (2003). The practice of social impact assessment-background. *Impact Assessment and Project Appraisal, 21*(2), 84–88.

Burt, R. S. (2001). Structural holes versus network closure as social capital. In N. Lin, K. S. Cook, & R. S. Burt (Eds.), *Social capital: Theory and research* (pp. 31–56). New York, NY: Aldine de Gruyter.

Burt, R. S., Hogarth, R. M., & Michaud, C. (2000). The social capital of French and American managers. *Organization Science, 11*(2), 123–147.

Calton, J. M., & Lad, L. J. (1995). Social contracting as a trust-building process of network governance. *Business Ethics Quarterly, 5*(2), 271–295.

Calton, J. M., & Payne, S. L. (2003). Coping with paradox: Multistakeholder learning dialogue as a pluralist sensemaking process for addressing messy problems. *Business & Society, 42*(1), 7–42.

Cardenas, J.-C. (2002). Rethinking local commons dilemmas: Lessons from experimental economics in the field. In J. Isham, T. Kelly, & S. Ramaswamy (Eds.), *Social capital and economic development: Well-being in developing countries* (pp. 138–155). Cheltenham, UK: Edward Elgar.

Carrin, G. J. (2006). Rousseau's "social contract": Contracting ahead of its time? *Bulletin of the World Health Organization, 84*(11), 917–918.

Caledonia land claim historical timeline. (2006, November 1). *CBC News.* Retrieved from http://www.cbc.ca

Cepiku, D. (2008, September). Small is (no longer) beautiful, network is. But can you manage it? Evidence from local government networks in the Lazio Region. *PUBLIC: Newsletter of the Institute of Public Governance & Management, 16.* Retrieved from http://www.esade.edu/public/modules.php?name=news&idnew=453&idissue=42&newlang=english

Coleman, J. S. (1959). Relational analysis: The study of social organizations with survey methods. *Human Organization, 17*(4), 28–36.

Coleman, J. S. (1988). Social capital in the creation of human capital [Supplement]. *American Journal of Sociology, 94,* S95–S120.

Collective Wisdom Initiative. (n.d.). Appreciative inquiry. Retrieved from http://www.collectivewisdominitiative.org/papers/pioneers_dialogue/04_apprec.pdf

Cooperrider, D. L., & Whitney, D. (2005). *Appreciative inquiry: A positive revolution in change.* San Francisco, CA: Berrett-Koehler.

Cross, R., & Thomas, R. J. (2009). *Driving results through social networks: How top organizations leverage networks for performance and growth.* San Francisco, CA: Jossey-Bass.

Cross, R. L., Thomas, R. J., & Light, D. A. (2009). How "who you know" affects what you decide. *Sloan Management Review, 50*(2), 35–42.

Crystallex International. (2011, February 6). Press release: Crystallex updates status of Las Cristinas Mine operating contract. Retrieved from http://www.crystallex.com

Delhey, J., & Newton, K. (2005). Predicting cross-national levels of social trust: Global pattern or Nordic exceptionalism. *European Sociological Review, 21*(4), 311–327.

de Waal, F. (2000). *Chimpanzee politics.* Baltimore, MD: Johns Hopkins University Press.

Diani, M. (2003). Networks and social movements: A research programme. In M. Diani & D. McAdam (Eds.), *Social movements and networks: Relational approaches to collective action* (pp. 299–319). Oxford, UK: Oxford University Press.

Dollar, D. (2005). Globalization, poverty, and inequality since 1980. *The World Bank Research Observer, 20*(2), 145–175.

Donaldson, T., & Dunfee, T. W. (1994). Towards a unified conception of business ethics: Integrative social contracts theory. *Academy of Management Review, 19*(2), 252–284.

Driscoll, C., & Starik, M. (2004). The primordial stakeholder: Advancing the conceptual consideration of stakeholder status for the natural environment. *Journal of Business Ethics, 49*(1), 55–73.

Eddy, M., & Baetz, J. (2010, November 25). Euro will survive debt crisis, Merkel vows. *Businessweek.* Retreived from http://www.businessweek.com/ap/financial news/D9JNB2PG0.htm

Edelenbos, J., & Klijn, E. H. (2007). Trust in complex decision-making networks: A theoretical and empirical exploration. *Administration & Society, 39*(1), 25–50.

Eno, R. (2010). The Confucian school. Retrieved from http://www.indiana.edu /~p374/Confucian_School.pdf

Evans, S. (2008, September 8). Settlement reached over Tata plant, problem may not be entirely solved. *Motor Trend.* Retrieved from http://wot.motor trend.com

Farmers block roads in Singur over Tata car plant. (2008, February 8). *Thaindian News.* Retrieved from http://www.thaindian.com

Fassin, Y. (2009). Inconsistencies in activists' behaviours and the ethics of NGOs. *Journal of Business Ethics, 90*(4), 503–521.

Finegold, M. A., Holland, B. M., & Lingham, T. (2002). Appreciative inquiry and public dialogue: An approach to community change. *Public Organization Review: A Global Journal, 2*, 235–252.

For Macaques, male bonding is a political move. (2010, November 18). *Science Daily.* Retrieved from http://www.sciencedaily.com/releases/2010/11 /101118124155.htm

Freeman, R. E. (1984). *Strategic management: A stakeholder approach.* Boston, MA: Pitman.

Freeman, R. E. (1994). The politics of stakeholder theory: Some future directions. *Business Ethics Quarterly, 4*(4), 409–421.

Freeman, R. E., & Evan, W. M. (1990). Corporate governance: A stakeholder interpretation. *Journal of Behavioral Economics, 19*(4), 337–359.

Freeman, R. E., Harrison, J. S., Wicks, A. C., Parmar, B. L., & de Colle, S. (2010). *Stakeholder theory: The state of the art*. Cambridge, UK: Cambridge University Press.

Friedkin, N. E. (1991). Theoretical foundations for centrality measures. *American Journal of Sociology, 96*(6), 1478.

Friedman, M. (1970). The social responsibility of business is to increase its profits. *New York Times, 32*–33, 122, 124–126.

Gamson, W. A. (1997). Constructing social protest. In S. M. Buechler & F. K. Cylke Jr. (Eds.), *Social movements: Perspectives and issues* (pp. 228–244). Mountain View, CA: Mayfield Publishing

Gargiulo, M., & Benassi, M. (2000). Trapped in your own net? Network cohesion, structural holes, and the adaptation of social capital. *Organization Science, 11*(2), 183–196.

The gas companies give their pitches. (1976, June 5). The Berger Pipeline Inquiry. *CBC Digital Archives*. Retrieved from http://archives.cbc.ca/society/native_issues/topics/295/

Gittell, R., & Vidal, A. (1998). *Community organizing: Building social capital as a development strategy*. Thousand Oaks, CA: Sage.

Glanville, J. L., & Bienenstock, E. J. (2009). A typology for understanding the connections among different forms of social capital. *American Behavioral Scientist, 52*(11), 1507–1530.

Goldsmith, S., & Eggers, W. D. (2004). *Governing by network: The new shape of the public sector*. Washington, DC: Brookings Institution Press.

Goffman, E. (1974). *Frame analysis*. Cambridge, MA: Harvard University Press.

Gould, R. V., & Fernandez, R. M. (1989). Structures of mediation: A formal approach to brokerage in transaction networks. *Sociological Methodology, 19*, 89–126.

Gray, B. (1989). *Collaborating: Finding common ground for multiparty problems*. San Francisco, CA: Jossey-Bass.

Gray, B., & Hay, T. M. (1986). Political limits to interorganizational consensus and change. *Journal of Applied Behavioral Science, 22*(2), 95–112.

Gray Gricar, B., & Brown, L. D. (1981). Conflict, power, and organization in a changing community. *Human Relations, 34*(10), 877–893.

Habermas, J. (1984). *The theory of communicative action* (2 vols.). Boston, MA: Beacon Press.

Haigh, N., & Griffiths, A. (2009). The natural environment as a primary stakeholder: The case of climate change. *Business Strategy & the Environment, 18*(6), 347–359.

Hanneman, R. A., & Riddle, M. (2011). *Introduction to social network methods*. Riverside, CA: University of California. Retrieved from http://faculty.ucr.edu/~hanneman/nettext/

Hardin, G. (1968). The tragedy of the commons. *Science, 162*, 1243–1248.

Harvey, K. J. (n.d.). Walmart sucks. Retrieved from http://walmartsucks.org/

Hawthorn, T. (2011, March 30). For sale: House where Greenpeace was born. Retrieved from http://tomhawthorne.blogspot.com/

Helliwell, J. F. (2006). Well-being, social capital, and public policy: What's new? *The Economic Journal, 116*(510), C34–C45.

Helliwell, J. F., & Putnam, R. D. (1999). Economic growth and social capital in Italy. In P. Dasgupta & I. Serageldin (Eds.), *Social capital: A multifaceted perspective*. New York, NY: World Bank.

Hill, R. A., & Dunbar, R. I. M. (2003). Social network size in humans. *Human Nature, 14*(1), 53–72.

Human, S. E., & Provan, K. G. (2000). Legitimacy building in the evolution of small-firm multilateral networks: A comparative study of success and demise. *Administrative Science Quarterly, 45*(2), 327–365.

Inglehart, R., & Baker, W. E. (2000). Modernization, cultural change, and the persistence of traditional values. *American Sociological Review, 65*(1), 19–55.

Inkpen, A. C., & Tsang, E. W. K. (2005). Social capital, networks, and knowledge transfer. *Academy of Management Review, 30*(1), 146–165.

International Network for Social Network Analysis. (n.d.). Retrieved from http://www.insna.org/

Isaacs, W. N. (1999). *Dialogue: The art of thinking together*. New York, NY: Doubleday.

Janis, I. L. (1972). *Victims of groupthink*. Boston, MA: Houghton Mifflin Company.

Johnson-Cramer, M., Parise, S., & Cross, R. L. (2007). Managing change through networks and values. *California Management Review, 49*(3), 85–109.

Jones, C., Hesterly, W. S., & Borgatti, S. P. (1997). A general theory of network governance: Exchange conditions and social mechanisms. *Academy of Management Review, 22*(4), 911–945.

Joyce, S., & Thomson, I. (2000). Earning a social licence to operate: Social acceptability and resource development in Latin America. *The Canadian Mining and Metallurgical Bulletin, 93*(1037), 49–52.

Kennard, M. (2010, June 1). China suitors' deep pockets hold hope for small miners. *Financial Times*. Retrieved from http://www.ft.com

Knoke, D. (2009). Playing well together: Creating corporate social capital in strategic alliance networks. *American Behavioral Scientist, 52*(12), 1690–1708.

Krackhardt, D. (1990). Assessing the political landscape: Structure, cognition, and power in organizations. *Administrative Science Quarterly, 35*(2), 342–369.

Krebs, V. E. (2002). Mapping networks of terrorist cells. *Connections, 24*(3), 43–52.

Krishna, A. (2001). Moving from the stock of social capital to the flow of benefits: The role of agency. *World Development, 29*(3), 925–943.

Lincoln, J. R., & Miller, J. (1979). Work and friendship ties in organizations: A comparative analysis of relational networks. *Administrative Science Quarterly, 24*(2), 181–199.

Litz, R. A. (1996). A resource-based view of the socially responsible firm: Stakeholder interdependence, ethical awareness, and issue responsiveness as strategic assets. *Journal of Business Ethics, 15*(12), 1355–1363.

Lomnitz, L., & Pérez-Lizaur, M. (1987). *A Mexican elite family, 1820–1980.* Princeton, NJ: Princeton University Press.

Loury, G. (1977). A dynamic theory of racial income differences. In P. Wallace & A. LeMund (Eds.), *Women, minorities, and employment discrimination* (pp. 153–186). Lexington, MA: Lexington Books.

Maak, T. (2007). Responsible leadership, stakeholder engagement, and the emergence of social capital. *Journal of Business Ethics, 74*(4), 329–343.

Mackenzie Gas Project. (n.d.). Aboriginal Pipeline Group (APG). Retrieved from http://www.mackenziegasproject.com/whoWeAre/APG/APG.htm

Mackenzie Valley: 37 years of negotiation. (2011, January 11). *CBC News.* Retrieved from http://www.cbc.ca/news/business/story/2010/12/16/f-mackenzie-valley -pipeline-history.html

The Mackenzie Valley pipeline: FAQ. (2007, March 12). *CBC News.* Retrieved from http://www.cbc.ca/news/background/mackenzievalley_pipeline/faqs.html

Mahon, J. F., & Waddock, S. A. (1992). Strategic issues management: An integration of issue lifecycle perspectives. *Business & Society, 31*(1), 19.

Meuleman, L. (2010). The cultural dimension of metagovernance: Why governance doctrines may fail. *Public Organization Review, 10*(1), 49–70.

Miller, C. C., & Ireland, R. D. (2005). Intuition in strategic decision making: Friend or foe in the fast-paced 21st century? *Academy of Management Executive, 19*, 19–30.

Mitchell, R. K., Agle, B. R., & Wood, D. J. (1997). Toward a theory of stakeholder identification and salience: Defining the principle of who and what really counts. *Academy of Management Review, 22*(4), 853–886.

Molinas, J. (2002). The interactions of bonding, bridging, and linking dimensions of social capital: Evidence from rural Paraguay. In J. Isham, T. Kelly, & S. Ramaswamy (Eds.), *Social capital and economic development: Well-being in developing countries* (pp. 104–137). Cheltenham, UK: Edward Elgar.

Monterrico Metals (MNA). (2005, February 11). *Investor Chronicle.* Retrieved from http://www.investorchronicle.co.uk

Monterrico Metals company financial information (2011, January 3). *ADVFN.* Retrieved from http://www.advfn.com

Moran, P. (2005). Structural vs. relational embeddedness: Social capital and managerial performance. *Strategic Management Journal, 26*(12), 1129–1151.

Mouawad, J. (2009, June 8). Shell to pay $15.5 million to settle Nigerian case. *New York Times Online.* Retrieved from http://www.nytimes.com

Murray, W. E., & Overton, J. D. (2011). Neoliberalism is dead, long live neoliberalism? Neostructuralism and the international aid regime of the 2000s. *Progress in Development Studies, 11*(4), 307–319.

Nahapiet, J., & Ghoshal, S. (1998). Social capital, intellectual capital, and the organizational advantage. *Academy of Management Review, 23*(2), 242–266.

Narayan, D. (1999). Bonds and bridges: Social capital and poverty. In J. Isham, T. Kelly, & S. Ramaswamy (Eds.), *Social capital and economic development: Well-being in developing countries* (pp. 58–81). Cheltenham, UK: Edward Elgar.

Narayan, D., & Cassidy, M. F. (2001). A dimensional approach to measuring social capital: Development and validation of a social capital inventory. *Current Sociology, 49*(2), 59–102.

Nelsen, J., & Scoble, M. (2006, May). *Social license to operate: Issues of situational analysis and process.* Poster presented at the Canadian Institute of Mining Metallurgy and Petroleum conference, Vancouver, BC.

Norman, A. (1999). *Slam-dunking Wal-Mart.* Atlantic City, NJ: Raphel Marketing.

Norman, A. (2004). *The case against Wal-Mart.* Atlantic City, NJ: Raphel Marketing.

Nolan, D. (2010, November 21). Judge orders natives to halt blockades at Brantford construction sites. Retrieved from http://www.thespec.com

OECD. (2001). *The well-being of nations: The role of human and social capital.* Paris, France: Organization for Economic Co-operation and Development.

Oh, H., Labianca, G., & Chung, M.-H. (2006). A multilevel model of group social capital. *Academy of Management Review, 31*(3), 569–582.

Olson, J. C., & Reynolds, T. J. (1983). Understanding consumers' cognitive structures: Implications for advertising strategy. In L. Percy & A. G. Woodside (Eds.), *Advertising and consumer psychology* (pp. 77–90). Lexington, MA: Lexington Books.

Onyx, J., & Bullen, P. (2000). Measuring social capital in five communities. *Journal of Applied Behavioral Science, 36*, 23–42.

Orts, E. W., & Strudler, A. (2002). The ethical and environmental limits of stakeholder theory. *Business Ethics Quarterly, 12*(2), 215–233.

Orts, E. W., & Strudler, A. (2009). Putting a stake in stakeholder theory [Supplement 4]. *Journal of Business Ethics, 88*, 605–615.

Ostrom, E. (1990). *Governing the commons: The evolution of institutions for collective action.* Cambridge, UK: Cambridge University Press.

Ostrom, E., Ahn, T. K., & Olivares, C. (2003). Una perspective del capital social desde las ciencias socials: Capital social y accion colective. *Revista Mexicana de Sociología, 65*(1), 155–233.

Ouchi, W. G. (1980). Markets, bureaucracies, and clans. *Administrative Science Quarterly, 25*(1), 129–141.

Partners in Salford. (n.d.). Salford's future search conference. Retrieved from http://www.partnersinsalford.org/future-search-2.htm

Peru Industry: Revolt in the Andes. (2007, September 21). *Economist Intelligence Unit.* Retrieved from http://www.eiu.com

Petty, R. E., & Cacioppo, J. T. (1986). The elaboration likelihood model of persuasion. In L. Berkowitz (Ed.), *Advances in experimental social psychology* (Vol. 19, pp. 123–205). New York, NY: Academic Press.

Phelps, C. C. (2010). A longitudinal study of the influence of alliance network structure and composition on firm exploratory innovation. *Academy of Management Journal, 53*(4), 890–913.

Phillips, R. (2003). *Stakeholder theory and organizational ethics.* San Francisco, CA: Berrett-Koehler Publishers.

Phillips, R. A., & Reichart, J. (2000). The environment as a stakeholder? A fairness-based approach. *Journal of Business Ethics, 23*(2), 185–197.

Portes, A. (1998). Social capital: Its origins and applications in modern sociology. *Annual Review of Sociology, 24*(1), 1–24.

Portes, A. (2000). The two meanings of social capital. *Sociological Forum, 15*(1), 1–12.

Post, J. E., Lawrence, A. T., & Weber, J. (2002). *Business and society: Corporate strategy, public policy, ethics* (10th ed.). New York, NY: McGraw-Hill.

Post, J. E., Preston, L. E., & Sachs, S. (2002). *Redefining the corporation: Stakeholder management and organizational wealth.* Stanford, CA: Stanford University Press.

Powell, W. W. (1990). Neither markets nor hierarchy: Network forms of organization. In B. M. Staw & L. L. Cummings (Eds.), *Research organizational behavior: An annual series of analytical essays and critical reviews* (12th ed., pp. 295–336). Greenwich, CT: JAI Press Inc.

Putnam, R. D. (2000). *Bowling alone: The collapse and revival of American community.* New York, NY: Simon & Schuster.

Regester, M., & Larkin, J. (2008). *Risk issues and crisis management in public relations: A casebook of best practice* (4th ed.). London, UK: Chartered Institute of Public Relations and Kogan Page.

Reich, R. B. (2007). *Supercapitalism: The transformation of business, democracy, and everyday life.* New York, NY: Alfred Knopf.

Reynolds, T. J., & Gutman, J. (1988). Laddering theory, method, analysis, and interpretation. *Journal of Advertising Research, 28*(1), 11–31.

Richter, U. (2010). Liberal thought in reasoning on CSR. *Journal of Business Ethics, 97*(4), 625–649.

Rio Blanco Torture: Investigation Incomplete. (2009, March 31). Peru Support Group. Retrieved from http://www.perusupportgroup.org.uk

Roberts, N. (2000). Wicked problems and network approaches to resolution. *International Public Management Review, 1*(1), 1–19.

Roloff, J. (2008). Learning from multi-stakeholder networks: Issue-focused stakeholder management. *Journal of Business Ethics, 82*(1), 233–250.

Romesburg, H. C. (2004). *Cluster analysis for researchers.* Raleigh, NC: Lulu Press.

Roseland, M. (2005). *Toward sustainable communities: Resources for citizens and their governments* (2nd ed.). Gabriola Island, BC: New Society Publishers.

Ross, M. L. (2001). Does oil hinder democracy? *World Politics, 53*(3), 325–361.

Rousseau, J.-J. (1968). *The social contract, or principles of political right* (M. Cranston, Trans.). London, UK: Penguin Books.

Rowley, T. J., Behrens, D., & Krackhardt, D. (2000). Redundant governance structures: An analysis of structural and relational embeddedness is the steel and semiconductor industries. *Strategic Management Journal, 21*(3), 369–386.

Russo, M. V., & Fouts, P. A. (1997). A resource-based perspective on corporate environmental performance and profitability. *Academy of Management Journal, 40*(3), 534–559.

Sachs, J. (2005). *The end of poverty: Economic possibilities of our time.* New York, NY: Penguin.

SAFEmap. (1999). *Safety culture survey report of the Australian Minerals Industry, July 1999.* Canberra, Australia: Minerals Council of Australia.

Salazar, C. (2009, June 6). Up to 36 reported killed in Amazon land protest. *The Nation on the Web*, Retrieved from http://www.nation.com.pk/pakistan-news-newspaper-daily   english-online/International/06-Jun-2009/Up-to-36-reported-killed-in-Amazon-land-protest

Saunders, D. (2011, June 25). Germany's season of angst: Why a prosperous nation is turning on itself. *The Globe and Mail.* Retrieved from http://www.theglobeandmail.com/news/world/europe/germanys-season-of-angst-why-a-prosperous-nation-is-turning-on-itself/article2075253/

Scherer, A. G., Palazzo, G., & Matten, D. (2009). The business firm as a political actor: A new theory of the firm for a globalized world. *Business & Society, 48*(4), 577–580.

Senge, P. (1990). *The fifth discipline: The art and practice of the learning organization.* New York, NY: Doubleday.

Senge, P., Kleiner, A., Roberts, C., Ross, R. B., & Smith, B. J. (1994). *The fifth discipline fieldbook: Strategies and tools for building a learning organization.* New York, NY: Currency/Doubleday.

Sharma, S., Vredenburg, H., & Westley, F. (1994). Strategic bridging: A role for the multinational corporation in Third World development. *Journal of Applied Behavioral Science, 30*(4), 458–476.

Smith, R. A., & Fink, E. L. (2010). Compliance dynamics within a simulated friendship network I: The effects of agency, tactic, and node centrality. *Human Communication Research, 36*(2), 232–260.

Snow, D. A., & Benford, R. D. (1992). Master frames and cycles of protest. In A. D. Morris & C. McClurg Mueller (Eds.), *Frontiers in social movement theory* (pp. 133–154). New Haven, CT: Yale University Press

Srivastava, M. (2008, August 27). Why Indian farmers are fighting Tata's Nano. *Businessweek.* Retrieved from http://www.businessweek.com

State smoking rates hit historic low. (2010, April 23). WANE-TV. Retrieved from http://www.wane.com

Steier, L. (2000). Entrepreneurship and the evolution of angel financial networks. *Organization Studies, 21*(1), 163–192.

Stevenson, M. (November 4, 2004). Despite months of protest, Wal-Mart owned store opens near Mexico's pyramids. *San Diego Union Tribune.* Retrieved from http://legacy.signonsandiego.com/news/mexico/20041104-1407-mexico-wal-mart-ruins.html

Stomer, F. (2003). Making the shift: Moving from "ethics pays" to an inter-systems model of business. *Journal of Business Ethics, 44*(4), 279–289.

The Strategy Board. (n.d.). Your city! Developing the vision updates. Retrieved from http://www.yourcityyoursay.com/your_city.php?news_uid=12

Stringer, N. (2007, April 4). Smoking cessation rates are up, cigarette consumption down, says UCSD study of California's tobacco control program. University of California–San Diego Health System. Retrieved from http://health.ucsd.edu

Strutzenberger, M. (2011, April 21). Achieving our "master narrative" through up-coming Cincinnati summit. Retrieved from http://appreciativeinquiry.case.edu/intro/pressDetail.cfm?coid=13780

Suchman, M. C. (1995). Managing legitimacy: Strategic and institutional approaches. *Academy of Management Review, 20*(3), 571–610.

Svendsen, A. C., & Laberge, M. (2005). Convening stakeholder networks: A new way of thinking, being and engaging. *Journal of Corporate Citizenship, 19,* 91–104.

Szreter, S., & Woolcock, M. (2004). Health by association? Social capital, social theory, and the political economy of public health. *International Journal of Epidemiology, 33*(4), 650–667.

Three workers died and several disappeared during an attack on Zijin's Rio Blanco. (2009, November 9). *Mines and Communities.* Retrieved from http://www.minesandcommunities.org

Thomson, I., & Boutilier, R. G. (2011). Social license to operate. In P. Darling (Ed.), *SME mining engineering handbook* (pp. 1779–1796). Littleton, CO: Society for Mining, Metallurgy and Exploration.

Trist, E. (1983). Referent organizations and the development of inter-organizational domains. *Human Relations, 36*(3), 269–284.

Tsai, W., & Ghoshal, S. (1998). Social capital and value creation: The role of intrafirm networks. *Academy of Management Review, 41*(4), 464–476.

Tuckman, B. (1965). Developmental sequence in small groups. *Psychological Bulletin, 63*(6), 384–399.

Two die in attack on Chinese-owned mine in Peru (2009, November 2). *China Digital Times*. Retrieved from http://www.chinadigitaltimes.net

United Food and Commercial Workers International Union. (2011a). Making change at Walmart: Our communities, our future. Retrieved from http://makingchangeatwalmart.org/

United Food and Commercial Workers International Union. (2011b). Walmart watch. Retrieved from http://walmartwatch.org/

UPDATE 2: Monterrico Metals agrees to $186 mln bid from Zijin. (2007, October 26). *Reuters*. Retrieved from http://www.reuters.com

U.S. Energy Information Administration. (2009). Energy in brief: What everyone should know about energy. Retrieved from http://tonto.eia.doe.gov/energy_in_brief/world_oil_market.cfm

van Rekom, J., & Wierenga, B. (2007). On the hierarchical nature of means–end relationships in laddering data. *Journal of Business Research, 60*(4), 401–410.

Waddell, S. (2003). Global action networks: A global invention helping business make globalisation work for all. *Journal of Corporate Citizenship, 12*, 27–42.

Waddell, S. (2007). Realising global change: Developing the tools; building the infrastructure. *Journal of Corporate Citizenship, 26*, 69–84.

Wallerstein, I. (1979). *The capitalist world-economy*. Cambridge, UK: Cambridge University Press.

Wehmeier, S. (2006). The myth of rationality in public relations. *Public Relations Review, 32*, 213–220.

Weisbord, M. R., & Janoff, S. (1995). *Future search: An action guide to finding common ground in organizations & communities*. San Francisco, CA: Berrett-Koehler.

Westley, F., & Vredenburg, H. (1991). Strategic bridging: The collaboration between environmentalists and business in the marketing of green products. *Journal of Applied Behavioral Science, 27*(1), 65–90.

Wheeler, D., Fabig, H., & Boele, R. (2002). Paradoxes and dilemmas for stakeholder responsive firms in the extractive sector: Lessons from the case of Shell and the Ogoni. *Journal of Business Ethics, 39*(3), 297–318.

Wilson, C., & Wilson, P. (2006). *Make poverty business: Increase profits and reduce risk by engaging with the poor.* Sheffield, UK: Greenleaf.

Wood, D. J., & Gray, B. (1991). Toward a comprehensive theory of collaboration. *Journal of Applied Behavioral Science, 27*(2), 139–162.

Woodruff, R. B. (1997). Customer value: The next source of competitive advantage. *Journal of the Academy of Marketing Science, 25*(2), 139–153.

Woolcock, M. (2002). Social capital in theory and practice: Where do we stand? In J. Isham, T. Kelly, & S. Ramaswamy (Eds.), *Social capital and economic development: Well-being in developing countries* (pp. 18–39). Cheltenham, UK: Edward Elgar.

Index

Announcing the Business Expert Press Digital Library

Concise E-books Business Students
Need for Classroom and Research

This book can also be purchased in an e-book collection by your library as

- a one-time purchase,
- that is owned forever,
- allows for simultaneous readers,
- has no restrictions on printing,
- can be downloaded as PDFs from within the library community.

Our digital library collections are a great solution to beat the rising cost of textbooks. E-books can be loaded into their course management systems or onto students' e-book readers.

The **Business Expert Press** digital libraries are very affordable, with no obligation to buy in future years.

For more information, please visit **www.businessexpertpress.com/librarians**. To set up a trial in the United States, please contact **Sheri Dean** at sheri.dean@globalepress.com; for all other regions, contact **Nicole Lee** at *nicole.lee@igroupnet.com*.

OTHER TITLES IN OUR STRATEGIC MANAGEMENT COLLECTION
Collection Editors: **Mason Carpenter and William Q. Judge**

Building Strategy and Performance Through Time: The Critical Path by Kim Warren

A Leader's Guide to Knowledge Management: Drawing on the Past to Enhance Future Performance by John Girard and JoAnn L. Girard

An Executive's Primer on the Strategy of Social Networks by Mason Carpenter

Fundamentals of Global Strategy: A Business Model Approach by Cornelis de Kluyver

Strategic Analysis and Choice: A Structured Approach by Alfred Warner

Business Goes Virtual: Realizing the Value of Collaboration, Social and Virtual Strategies by John Girard, Cindy Gordon, and JoAnn L. Girard

CPSIA information can be obtained at www.ICGtesting.com
Printed in the USA
BVOW070043280912

301557BV00004B/5/P